D0193997

Dedication

To Daniel and Allison, who've taught me to see the world anew.

Your safety is your responsibility

Hiking and camping in the wilderness can be dangerous. Experience and preparation reduce risk, but will never eliminate it. The unique details of your specific situation and the decisions you make at that time will determine the outcome. This book is not a substitute for common sense or sound judgment. If you doubt your ability to negotiate mountain terrain, respond to wild animals, or handle sudden, extreme weather changes, hike only in a group led by a competent guide. The author and the publisher of this book disclaim liability for any loss or injury incurred by anyone using information in this book.

Yucca flowers with Point Mugu in the distance

50
BEST
SHORT HIKES
in
California's
Central Coast

John Krist

WILDERNESS PRESS
BERKELEY

917.94
c.1

Copyright © 1998 by John Krist
Photos and maps by the author
Design by Thomas Winnett and Kathy Morey
Front-cover photo: © 1998 by David Muench
Back-cover photos: © 1998 by John Krist
Cover design by Larry Van Dyke
Clip art adapted from Macromedia FreeHand 7 collection

Library of Congress Card Number 97-32838
ISBN 0-89997-202-0

Manufactured in the United States of America
Published by **Wilderness Press**
     2440 Bancroft Way
     Berkeley, CA 94704
     (800) 443-7227; FAX (510) 548-1355
     Email wpress@ix.netcom.com

     Write, call or email us for free catalog
     Visit us at www.wildernesspress.com

Front cover: **Anacapa Island, Channel Islands National Park**
Back cover: **Island Buckwheat, San Miguel Island** *(top)*;
      Morro Rock, Morro Bay State Park *(bottom)*.

Library of Congress Cataloging-in-Publication Data

Krist, John, 1958–
     50 best short hikes in California's Central Coast / by John Krist.
          p.   cm.
     Includes bibliographical references (p.) and index.
     ISBN 0-89997-202-0
     1. Hiking--California--Pacific Coast--Guidebooks. 2. Pacific Coast (Calif.)--
Guidebooks. I. Title.
GV199.42.C22C334 1998
917.94'910453--dc21   97-32838
                                                  CIP

Contents

Contents

Summary of this book's hikes

Hike	Distance	Difficulty	Child Rating	Principal Attraction
Part 1: Trails of Channel Islands National Park				
1	1.8 miles	Easy	5 and up	Wildlife, scenery
2	3.6 miles	Moderate	5 and up	Caliche forest, wildlife
3	6 miles	Moderate	5 and up	Views
4	14 miles	Moderate	10 and up	Sea lion rookery, views
5	2.5 miles	Easy	10 and up	Views, wildlife
6	0.25 miles	Easy	10 and up	Views, wildlife
7	3.2 miles	Moderate	10 and up	Views, wildlife
8	3.3 miles	Moderate	10 and up	Views. wildlife
9	2.2 miles	Easy	5 and up	Views, historical artifacts
10	6 miles	Easy	10 and up	Historical artifacts, wildlife
11	4.8 miles	Moderate	10 and up	Views. historical artifacts
12	7 miles	Moderate	10 and up	Views, geological formations
13	4 miles	Moderate	5 and up	Views, beach
14	3.6 miles	Moderate	5 and up	Views
15	5.7 miles	Moderate	10 and up	Views, Torrey pine forest
Part 2: Trails of Los Padres National Forest				
16	5 miles	Moderate	10 and up	Views, stream
17	3.5 miles	Moderate	10 and up	Views, guided nature trail
18	3.2 miles	Easy	5 and up	Stream, wildlife
19	6 miles	Strenuous	10 and up	Views, historical artifacts, stream
20	3.4 miles	Easy	5 and up	Views, pioneer cabin site
21	6 mile	Strenuous	10 and up	Views, hot springs
22	3 miles	Moderate	10 and up	Views
23	3.4 miles	Moderate	10 and up	Views, stream
24	2 miles	Easy	5 and up	Views, stream
25	5.8 miles	Strenuous	10 and up	Views, pine grove
26	4 miles	Easy	5 and up	Stream, wildlife, geological formations
27	11.2 miles	Strenuous	10 and up	Views
28	2.2 miles	Easy	5 and up	Views, wildlife
29	0.6 mile	Easy	3 and up	Waterfall
30	6.2 miles	Easy	5 and up	Stream, waterfall, forest
31	5.6 miles	Moderate	10 and up	Geological formations, rock art, stream
32	1 mile	Easy	5 and up	Stream, wildlife
Part 3: Trails of Montaña de Oro, Morro Bay and Nipomo Dunes				
33	2.4 miles	Moderate	5 and up	Views, wildlife
34	2 miles	Easy	5 and up	Views, geological formations
35	1.2 miles	Easy	5 and up	Views, historical artifacts
36	3.4 miles	Easy	5 and up	Views, wildlife
37	3.4 miles	Easy	5 and up	Sand dunes, views, wildlife
38	8 miles	Strenuous	10 and up	Views, stream, wildlife
39	10 miles	Moderate	10 and up	Wildlife, beach, views
40	7.5 miles	Moderate	10 and up	Views, wildlife, stream
41	1.7 miles	Easy	5 and up	Stream, wildlife
42	2.2 miles	Easy	3 and up	Lake, dunes, wildlife, wildflowers
Part 4: Trails of Santa Monica Mountains National Recreation Area				
43	3.5 miles	Easy	5 and up	Views, geological formations
44	7.5 miles	Moderate	10 and up	Fossils, stream, views, wildflowers
45	5.5 miles	Moderate	10 and up	View
46	9.7 miles	Strenuous	10 and up	Views, stream, wildlife
47	7 miles	Strenuous	10 and up	Views, stream. geological formations
48	1.5 miles	Easy	5 and up	Views, reconstructed Chumash village
49	4.3 miles	Moderate	10 and up	Views, wildflowers
50	3.2 miles	Easy	5 and up	Views, old ranch site

Introduction

On the cultural landscape of California, the Central Coast region stands distinct, neither so densely urban as the great Southern California metropolis that abuts it on the south nor as cluttered with resort towns and tourist attractions as the region from Monterey north. In climate and geography it likewise stands apart, a transition zone straddling the divide between the well-watered northern part of the state and the arid south, a place where mountains run the wrong way, snow falls within sight of the sea and cactus grows on sandy slopes kissed by salt-tangy fog.

It is, for the purposes of this book, the region lying within 30 miles of the ocean in Ventura, Santa Barbara and San Luis Obispo counties, bordered on the north by the wild, forested mountains of the Big Sur country and on the south by the arid land beyond the Tehachapis. There is a rich diversity of topography, wildlife and cultural resources in this Tri-Counties region: ancient Chumash pictographs, California condor habitat, coastal sage scrub, chaparral, snow-capped peaks forested by big-cone spruce, islands inhabited by rare endemic plants and animals, vast coastal dune systems, marshes, tidepools and streams.

The human population rests lightly on this land, even though it contains some of the oldest communities in California. The biggest cities are small by contemporary standards; ranching and farming still dominate the inhabited strip along the ocean and in the inland valleys, often tied to communities grown up around 18th-century Spanish missions — which in turn were typically built on the location of native villages. Much of the remaining terrain lies within the boundaries of state and federal park lands, which preserve a remarkable diversity of natural and cultural resources. Most are within a few hours' drive of even the major urban areas of Southern California, and are thus well suited to day trips.

This guide focuses on hikes in the most noteworthy of these natural areas: the south half of Los Padres National Forest, a sprawling preserve draped across the mountains of the Transverse Ranges; Channel Islands National Park, a unique string of windswept islands reaching west from the Santa Barbara-Ventura coastline; the Santa Monica Mountains National Recreation Area, a patchwork of state and federal properties preserving a

1

host of dwindling ecosystems within a few miles of the state's largest urban area; Morro Bay State Park, a rare combination of coastal marshes, estuaries and oak woodlands; Guadalupe–Nipomo Dunes Preserve, a vast expanse of coastal dunes interlaced with wetlands; and Montaña de Oro State Park, a sweep of hills cut by streams that empty into the Pacific along a craggy shoreline dotted with tidepools.

Using This Book

This book is designed to aid visitors whose time is limited or who are accompanied by children. The 50 hikes described in its pages sample the region's popular attractions, but also take you to out-of-the-way corners of wilderness you might otherwise miss. The hikes have been selected to offer a maximum return for a moderate investment in time and effort. They range from easy nature trails that can be walked in an hour even by young children, to more challenging routes suitable for a long day hike.

Within each section, the hikes are listed alphabetically. Precise directions to the trailheads are provided, as well as information about camping, visitor centers, and the availability of water, parking and restrooms.

Each section opens with an overview of the area's human and geological history, as well as the flora and fauna you're likely to encounter, in the hope that such information will make your hikes more satisfying. It is not within the scope of this book, however, to present an extensive or detailed guide to any of those subjects. For readers interested in exploring the subjects in greater depth, a list of recommended reading is at the end of the book.

Each trail description is preceded by a summary listing the mileage from start to finish (not the one-way distance), level of difficulty, starting elevation, highest or lowest point on the trail, and United States Geological Survey topographic map or maps covering the area. Most of the hikes in this guide do not exceeds 10 miles, which in the author's experience is the limit for a pleasant, casually paced day afoot.

As a special aid for hikers with children, each trail has been assigned a "child rating" that gives the minimum age at which a youngster might reasonably be expected to complete the hike under his or her own power. In general, easy nature trails of a mile or less are considered suitable for kids three and up, while those of 1 to 5 miles that do not involve strenuous climbs are rated for youngsters five and older. For the purposes of this book, hikes of more than 5 miles, and shorter trips that include steep ascents, are considered suitable only for children 10 and older. These mileage ratings are conservative, and are based on the author's personal experience and on the recommendations of pediatricians and child-development experts.

In the case of hikes on the Channel Islands, the condition of the trail is not the governing factor; the rigors of the boat ride and landing are. Long channel crossings and difficult landings through rough surf or onto precarious ladders are generally beyond the capabilities of children much younger than 10, and the ratings for those hikes have been adjusted accordingly.

Regardless of the rating, keep in mind that children vary greatly in stamina, determination and distractibility. A hike that would prove easy for one five-year-old might as well be an ascent of Mt. Whitney for another child of the same age, whereas a motivated and energetic seven-year-old may be able to complete any hike in this book. View the guide as only a rough estimation, prepare to move slowly, and be ready to turn back at any time even if you haven't reached your objective—unless you don't mind hiking back to your car or campsite with a cranky or sleeping child on your shoulders.

Trail Etiquette

To keep damage to a minimum, please observe a few elementary rules when hiking.

1. Pack out your trash. It shouldn't be necessary to remind anyone of this. Still, every backcountry traveler has come across soft-drink cans, film containers, candy wrappers or worse on the trail. If you can carry it in, you can certainly carry it out. Some hikers, in fact, make it a point to carry out more than they carried in, cleaning up after their less thoughtful fellow travelers.

2. Be respectful toward your fellow foot-travelers. Let faster-moving parties pass, keep noise to a minimum, acknowledge the desire for solitude that sends many people into the wilderness in the first place. Obey regulations, which in many areas prohibit pets, vehicles (including bicycles) and firearms or other weapons on the trails.

3. Leave everything as you found it. It is illegal to disturb plants or wildlife in most areas under federal or state jurisdiction, or to remove archaeological artifacts, dead wood, fossils or other geological features. If you must carry away a memento of your visit, make sure it's only a photograph. This is particularly important on the Channel Islands, where there are many exposed archaeological sites and where the rare, native plants are desperately vulnerable to damage. Wildlife in the islands is also uniquely susceptible to disturbance, and all rules must be rigidly enforced if the fragile ecosystems there are to remain in their remarkable state.

Hiking Safety

Even if you plan to spend no more than a few hours on the trail, you should observe a few elementary, common-sense precautions. Few of these trails will take you far from civilization, but each year hikers in these relatively tame wildlands become lost, suffer from exposure and require rescuing because they misjudged their abilities or failed to prepare.

1. Tell someone where you're going. Leave a precise description of your route with someone at home, and tell them when you plan to return. Do not deviate from that plan. If you get in trouble, searchers won't be able to find you unless you're where you were supposed to be.

2. Don't hike alone. Wilderness travel is always a risky undertaking; a misstep and a badly twisted or broken ankle can turn even a short day hike into a life-threatening experience. If you have a companion, one of you will be able to seek help. Solo travel has its charms, but it is only for the most experienced and self-reliant of backcountry travelers.

3. Prepare for the weather. Conditions change rapidly in the mountains, and a soaking fog can rapidly close in on travelers along the coast. Although conditions are unlikely to become life-threatening, it is always prudent to carry extra clothing that will keep you warm when wet. Conversely, some of these hikes traverse countryside that is torrid in the summer, in which case light-colored clothing and a sun hat will be more useful. On trips to the islands, visitors may encounter soaking sea spray, howling winds, dense fog and blistering sun — all on a single day trip. Dress in layers and be prepared for anything.

4. Know where you're going. The trails described in this book are fairly easy to follow. Still, you'll get more out of your hike if you study your route beforehand, carry this guide with you and bring the appropriate topographic map, which is listed in each trail description. The map and a compass — plus the ability to use them — will help you identify landmarks visible as you travel, which adds greatly to the enjoyment of a hike. They'll also help to keep you from getting lost — something that detracts greatly from the enjoyment of a hike.

5. Don't overdo it. The hikes in this book are geared toward the average hiker in decent physical condition, not triathletes or marathon-runners. Set a comfortable pace and you'll get where you're going without any problem.

6. Equip yourself properly. Pack snacks for quick energy. Carry plenty of water — an average person needs a gallon a day in hot weather. Carry a first-aid kit. Dress appropriately for the weather. And bring this guide.

Hiking With Children

Hiking poses special challenges when children are among your companions. Some of those challenges are physical, others are psychological. In both cases, it pays to be prepared.

In general, a baby is old enough to be carried on a hike when it can hold up its head without difficulty, something most infants are capable of by the

Author's daughter at Piedra Blanca, Hike #31

age of six months. In some ways, this is the best age at which to bring children on the trail, mainly because they'll sleep much of the time, they don't weigh much and they'll stay where you put them when you stop for a lunch break or an hour of wool-gathering at a spectacular viewpoint. On the other hand, an infant isn't very good at conversation and is decidedly unawed by scenery. Each age brings with it a unique combination of advantages and disadvantages.

There are several lightweight child-carriers on the market which will allow you to carry an infant in relative comfort even on a long day hike. Their thin shoulder pads and belts are not adequate, however, once the child reaches about 20 pounds. For toddlers you'll need a heavier pack, one designed—like any good internal- or external-frame backpack—to transfer most of the weight to your hips. Several models of these heavier child-carriers are available, although they are costly. Shop carefully, or inquire about rentals. Look for strong construction, plenty of adjustability to ensure your child won't outgrow it quickly, ample padding in the shoulder straps and hip belt, and storage for the many items you'll need to carry. Take time in the store to try it out with a real kid on board. Both of you need to be happy with the pack if you hope to enjoy your hikes.

Children develop at different rates, so it is risky to generalize. But you can probably count on carrying your youngster on most hikes until the age of three. After that, you'll need the pack for trails longer than a couple of miles, and those that involve much elevation change. From five on, with judicious trip selection, your child should be able to make it most of the way on his or her own.

Even if you are an experienced backpacker, carrying a child on your back will pose new challenges. For one thing, 30 pounds of kid does not behave like 30 pounds of tent, stove, sleeping bag, cookset and clothing. Kids move, throwing you off balance at critical moments. As cargo, a seated child has a lower center of gravity than a well-packed load of inanimate objects, making it almost impossible to achieve ideal weight distribution. Practice by carrying the child around town before venturing into the unpredictable backcountry.

There are a few other things to keep in mind when preparing to take your child on the trail.

1. Pack snacks such as bite-size pieces of fruit, raisins and crackers in small plastic bags so your child can munch as you walk. This will help prevent fussiness in a child riding in a pack, and will give an energy boost to one on foot. Don't wait more than half an hour into the hike to provide a child on foot with something to eat, or you'll risk the crankiness that comes with depleted blood sugar.

2. Bring spare diapers and a sealable plastic bag in which to store them when they're soiled. Do not bury disposables.

3. Remember to stop every hour or so and remove your child from the pack. A toddler will need to run around a bit, and an infant will welcome the change in position.

4. Apply sunscreen to your child, keeping in mind that shade is rare or nonexistent on the Channel Islands and other coastal parks.

5. If the weather is cold, keep your child bundled up. You might not be cold, but a child kept motionless in a backpack will become chilled long before you do.

6. If the weather is hot, a T-shirt and shorts are probably all you'll need to dress your child in. Hemmed in by the unbreathable nylon of most pack cloth, your youngster may have trouble staying cool. A hat is a good idea, although it's a rare child who won't send it sailing into the underbrush. Clamping a small umbrella to the pack frame to provide shade is a good idea, too, if you're hiking in open country.

7. Establish safety rules for your child. Before taking a youngster on a hike, make sure you discuss the importance of halting and remaining on the trail in the unlikely event you become separated. Dress your child in bright colors to make him or her easier to spot. Consider providing a plastic whistle the child can use to summon help. Emphasize the danger of sticking hands and feet into rocky crevices that might harbor snakes, scorpions or spiders, and caution against turning over rocks for the same reason. If there are several members in your party, designate one adult to lead the way and scout the trail for obstacles. Designate another adult to act as "sweeper" to bring up the rear and make sure no youngster falls too far behind.

8. Scale back your expectations. Whether your child is riding on your back or tramping at your side, he or she will determine the pace. Some youngsters will plug along at a good clip or ride uncomplainingly for hours in a backpack, while others stop to examine in minute detail every stick, rock and bird feather they come across. Remember that young children are not goal-oriented, and cannot be urged along by promising a beautiful view around the next corner. Neither of you will enjoy the trip if you spend most of your time commanding your child to move faster or to sit still in the pack and keep quiet. Resign yourself to a slower pace than you are used to, and enjoy the natural inquisitiveness that children display whenever they encounter unfamiliar sights and sounds—even if it takes the form of unanswerable questions repeated insistently during a steep ascent that has robbed you of breath.

A Note About Maps

For the day hikes described in this book, topographic maps are recommended, even though this book itself contains maps that will guide you to the trailheads and give you a general idea of the surrounding features.

Each trip description identifies the relevant 7.5′ topographic quadrangles produced by the United States Geological Survey, which provide details about terrain that the maps published in this book omit in the interest of clarity. The 7.5′ maps have replaced the old 15′ USGS maps, which covered an area 15 minutes of latitude by 15 minutes of longitude and for many years were the standard upon which backcountry travelers relied to identify features of the countryside and to anticipate the ups and downs of the trail. With their scale of about 1 mile to the inch, the 15′ series provided adequate detail and still covered a large area, so it was seldom necessary to carry more than one or two maps on any but the longest trips.

The Geological Survey, however, has discontinued publication of most of the 15′ maps. Instead, the government has updated the map data and switched to a series of 7.5′ quadrangles, which have a scale of 0.38 mile to the inch in the area covered by this book.

For some reason, however, many of the maps for areas described in this book are particularly outdated or inaccurate. In many cases, the trails are not depicted at all, while other manmade features such as roads have changed considerably. In those cases, the text offers advice on a superior substitute available from another source.

If your local sporting-goods store doesn't have what you need, USGS topographic maps may be ordered from the survey itself at:

U.S. Geological Survey
Box 25286, Federal Center
Denver, CO 80225

The Wilderness Press Map Centers also stock all the 7.5' maps for California, which may be either ordered from or purchased in person at the following addresses:

The Map Center
2440 Bancroft Way
Berkeley, CA 94704
Phone: (510) 841-MAPS

The Map Center
63 Washington St.
Santa Clara, CA 95050
Phone: (408) 296-MAPS   ■

IMPORTANT NOTE:

As this book was about to go to press (January 1998), the Destinet reservation system suspended operations. Until a new contract is signed, there will be no way to reserve space in state park campgrounds; all sites will be available on a first-come, first-served basis. The California Department of Parks and Recreation hope to have a new system in place by summer of 1998. For information about the current status of the state park reservation system, call the department at (916) 654-1066.

Skunk Point on Santa Rosa Island

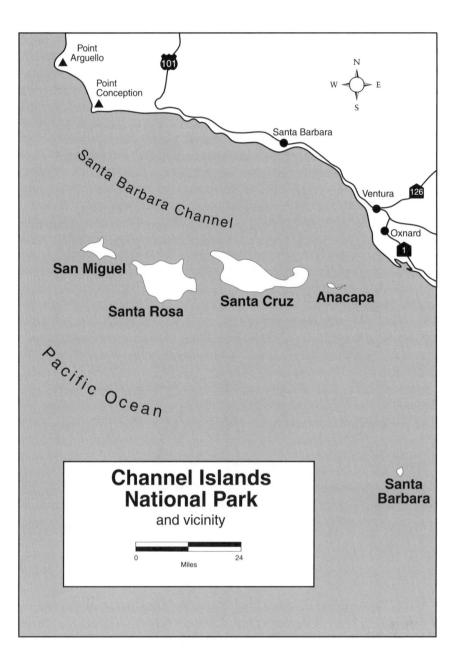

Point
Arguello ▲

US 101

Point
Conception ▲

N
W ◇ E
S

Santa Barbara ●

Ventura ● 126

Oxnard ●

1

Santa Barbara Channel

San Miguel

Santa Cruz

Anacapa

Santa Rosa

Pacific Ocean

**Channel Islands
National Park**
and vicinity

0   24
Miles

Santa
Barbara

Channel Islands National Park

Geological History

The Channel Islands rise like a dream from the sea, invisible much of the year from the mainland even though the nearest of them, Anacapa, is only 11 miles from shore. Coastal fog and haze hides them so frequently that even the original Chumash name for Anacapa — "eneepah" — means deception or mirage. When the fog lifts, however, or the offshore breeze dissipates the haze, the rugged islands stand out in bold relief against the horizon, startling even long-time residents of the Oxnard-Ventura area with their size and proximity.

Channel Islands National Park encompasses five islands, four of them (Anacapa, Santa Cruz, Santa Rosa and San Miguel) lying in a neat line from east to west off Point Mugu. The fifth, Santa Barbara, lies far to the south of the others. Together with San Clemente and San Nicolas (both owned by the Navy and off-limits to visitors) and Santa Catalina (a major and well-developed tourist attraction), they constitute what are known as the California Islands, all of which share a common, and complicated, origin and history.

The northern Channel Islands were once thought to be nothing more than a partially submerged extension of the Santa Monica Mountains, and some geology texts show them as having constituted a peninsula that extended west from Point Mugu and converted the Santa Barbara Channel into an enormous bay several million years ago. Belief in the existence of a now-vanished land bridge between the mainland and the islands had been encouraged by the discovery of fossil mammoth bones on Santa Rosa Island. Early researchers could find no other plausible explanation for their presence, and conjectured that ancestral mammoths — as well as other plant and animal species the islands share with the mainland — had crossed dry land and later been marooned by the rising sea.

More recent research, however, indicates that the ocean floor between the islands and the mainland lies too deep to have ever been uncovered during the ice ages. Other clues — the lack of mainland mammals such as mice and gophers, which would have eagerly filled suitable niches in the island ecology — also suggests the islands were never connected to the mainland. Detailed examination of the sea floor does show that the gap between the islands and the mainland dwindled to as little as 3 miles when the sea level reached its lowest point, a distance that such modern terrestrial mammals as elephants are known to swim.

The most widely accepted theory today is that the islands constitute the exposed highlands of a complex system of basins and ridges produced off the Central Coast by the same type of forces that produced the topography of the Basin and Range province of inland North America. Modern maps based on detailed soundings conducted over the years by oil companies and other researchers reveal that the sea floor in the Channel Islands area — a topographic province geologists refer to as the Continental Borderland — looks strikingly similar to the topography of eastern California's basin-and-range desert region.

The process of faulting and folding is thought to have taken place over the past 30 million years, linked to the movement of two of the great plates of the earth's crust, the Pacific Plate and the North American plate. The grinding passage of the Pacific plate, which is scraping past the North American plate on a slow journey northward, produces earthquakes and has thrust up a number of mountain ranges in Southern California.

The pressure also has crumpled the sea floor, warping it into a series of deep basins and high ridges. The islands, according to this theory, represent the exposed tops of these uplifted regions of sea floor. They comprise a variety of marine sediments, as well as volcanic rocks extruded during a period of igneous activity that built lava flows and undersea volcanoes in the channel from 24 million to 7 million years ago.

Fluctuating sea levels have over the years caused the exposed area of the islands to vary in shape and size. During the last ice age, which ended about 10,000 years ago, the four northern islands coalesced into a single land mass, which geologists call Santarosae; it dissolved again into separate islands when the ice melted and the sea rose.

The rock types exposed on the islands vary greatly. Santa Barbara and Anacapa are composed almost entirely of volcanic rock. San Miguel, Santa Rosa and Santa Cruz have volcanic foundations but are made up primarily of sandstone and shale; the softer rock has eroded into soils that support a much wider diversity of plant and animal life than is found on the more impoverished, erosion-resistant volcanic terrain of Anacapa and Santa Barbara.

Human History

The Channel Islands contain some of the oldest evidence of human habitation in California. Archaeological surveys indicate human presence on the islands more than 10,000 years ago, when the ancestors of the

Chumash established seasonal hunting and fishing camps on waterless Anacapa and Santa Barbara, and permanent settlements on the other three islands in the park.

The four northern islands contain hundreds of archaeological sites, ranging from simple middens — kitchen trash heaps filled with shells and animal bones —to burial grounds. Yielding a rich trove of artifacts, human remains and clues to diet and hunting practices, they have provided a wealth of information about early human occupancy. Some of the sites were plundered by amateur pot-hunters in the late 1800s, and others were later excavated by trained archaeologists. Still more have been identified but remain undisturbed.

San Miguel Island has more than 600 sites, some dating to 10,700 years ago. Santa Cruz contains at least 200. Santa Rosa has more than 160 documented sites; carbon dating techniques suggest an age of 40,000 years for one of them, based on charred bones and ash some researchers believe constitutes the remains of a cooking fire. Other archaeologists argue that it is more likely the result of a natural wildfire, presumably ignited by lightning, and cannot be regarded as evidence of such early human presence. An age of 40,000 years would predate the generally accepted occupancy period for California, which presupposes no human migration into the region until after the ice age had ended — no more than 11,000 to 12,000 years ago.

The early inhabitants of the islands, like their descendants up until the point of European contact, relied almost exclusively on the sea for their livelihood. Shellfish constituted the majority of their diet, supplemented by fish, wintering birds and the occasional sea mammal. Land animals, being rare, were seldom eaten.

Subsistence patterns changed about 4,000 years ago, as hunting of sea mammals — California sea lions, Steller sea lions, northern fur seals, northern elephant seals, harbor seals and sea otters — became much more important in the island economy. These animals congregate in great numbers on the northern islands, and could be taken with nothing more elaborate than a club. Plants provided some nutrition, but edible species were not particularly abundant on any of the islands and they never approached the dietary importance that they achieved on the mainland.

At the time of European contact in the 16th century, the islands were inhabited by a subgroup of the mainland Chumash known as the Island Chumash. The Chumash were one of the largest of California's native tribes, numbering as many as 30,000. At the time of European contact, they lived in 75 to 100 large villages scattered from Malibu Canyon in the Santa Monica Mountains on the south, to Morro Bay on the north, and inland as far as the western edge of the San Joaquin Valley.

Abalone shells and other debris in Chumash midden on San Miguel Island

The word "Chumash" is not what the people used to refer to themselves; it is a Spanish corruption of the name the mainland inhabitants used to refer to the natives on either Santa Cruz Island (*mitcúmac*) or Santa Rosa Island (*tcúmac*). It is probably derived from *alchum*, the word used by the residents of the Santa Barbara area for the shell beads that constituted a form of money, and meant "those who make shell beads." The beads were manufactured almost exclusively by the Island Chumash, from shells of the purple olivella snail.

Anthropologists have divided the Chumash into eight subgroups, based on geographic and linguistic differences: Obispeño, Purisimeño, Cuyama, Ynezeño, Barbareño, Emigdiano, Ventureño and Island. All spoke one of six branches in the Chumashan branch of the Hokan language family, which they shared with the Shastan, Karok, Yana and Pomo of Northern California, their neighbors the Salinan and Esselen just up the coast, and the Yuman of the Southern California desert

At the time of European contact, the Island Chumash are estimated to have numbered about 2,000. Like their mainland neighbors, with whom they carried on an extensive trade, they had a relatively simple material culture. They fashioned fish hooks of abalone or mussel shell, carved bowls and ritual objects from steatite (a soft rock also known as soapstone), wove fishing nets from plant fibers, and used spears or clubs to kill large animals such as sea lions and seals. They used caves and overhangs for shelter, and built simple domelike shelters of brush and tree limbs. Clothing, especially among men, was sparse. Through trade, they were able to acquire food and raw materials — meat, hides, grains and fruits — from the mainland to supplement the islands' natural resources.

Perhaps the most remarkable of Chumash technological achievements was the seagoing plank canoe, or *tomol*, which could be up to 30 feet long and could carry up to 4,000 pounds. Typically crewed by six men using double-bladed paddles, a *tomol* could accommodate up to 12 people and could be propelled through the water as fast as a man could run. It sometimes took six months to build one of these unusual craft — the boards had to be split laboriously from driftwood logs, and then drilled, sanded with sharkskin, stitched together and sealed with tar — and ownership of one was a mark of wealth.

The European period commenced on Oct. 10, 1542, when a pair of Spanish ships commanded by explorer Juan Cabrillo sailed into the Santa Barbara Channel and dropped anchor. Cabrillo and his men provided the first known written account of the California coast, sailing from Mexico north to Oregon and visiting most of the prominent coastal sites from San Diego to Mendocino. In the course of their exploration they landed on Santa Cruz, Santa Rosa and San Miguel islands, and reported in some detail about

The Cabrillo monument on San Miguel Island

the culture of the Island Chumash. They also visited and described mainland Chumash settlements in the Santa Barbara-Ventura region.

Cabrillo and his men are believed to have wintered that year on either San Miguel or Santa Rosa, where the expedition leader suffered an injury in a fall that led to his death on Jan. 3, 1543. He is believed to have been buried on one of the islands, although his grave has never been located. A monument to him was erected on San Miguel in 1937, on the 394th anniversary of his death, by the Cabrillo Civic Clubs of California. Later biographers, relying on Cabrillo's maps, believe the crew actually wintered on Santa Catalina Island and suggest it is the real resting place of the explorer.

Other seagoing expeditions followed, and in the late 1700s Russian, British and American fur traders entered the area in search of sea otters, which they hunted nearly to extinction. These visits were transitory, but they introduced unfamiliar diseases that greatly reduced the Island Chumash population. Natives were also frequent victims of violence at the hands of the newcomers.

Still, the most significant effect of European contact on the island residents would not come for nearly two centuries after Cabrillo's expedition, with the arrival of the first permanent settlers in the Central Coast region.

In 1782, Franciscan missionaries established a mission they called San Buenaventura, near the mouth of the Ventura River at the site of a large Chumash village. Four years later they established another mission at Santa Barbara, followed by La Purísima Concepción, near present-day Lompoc, in 1787. The settlements were among a chain of 21 the religious order established in partnership with the Spanish military throughout California between 1769 and 1823. Each was separated from the next by a day's journey, about 30 miles, along the coastal route between San Diego and San Francisco that became known as El Camino Real, The King's Road.

The purpose of the missions was twofold: They provided a mechanism to advance the conversion of the native population to Christianity, and they established a framework of self-sufficient communities knitting together, however tenuously, the northern frontier of Spain's North American possessions.

As they did wherever they established missions, the Spanish disrupted the traditional social structure and living arrangements of the mainland Chumash. Villages were depopulated, often under threat of force, and the residents moved into pestilential quarters on the mission grounds. Adults were forced to labor for the mission's soldiers and priests, helping to grow food, construct buildings and produce a variety of goods needed for trade and for use by the settlements. Chumash adolescents were removed into dormitories, segregated by sex, and subjected to religious indoctrination.

The ocean provided the Island Chumash no insulation from the Spanish Mission influence. Residents of the northern islands were forcibly removed to the mainland in the early 1800s and brought into the mission settlements at Santa Barbara, Ventura and La Purísima.

As it did to natives throughout California, the mission system quickly and systematically destroyed first the culture of the Chumash and then the population itself. Forced to give up their own religious practices, prevented from establishing traditional family, clan and village social structures, exposed to virulent diseases to which they had no immunity, the Chumash dwindled quickly. The native population of California dropped from 300,000 to about 30,000 by the early 19th century, and population losses among the Chumash reached similar proportions.

The void created on the islands by removal of the native inhabitants was soon filled. Following Mexico's independence from Spain in 1822, the government begin the practice of rewarding loyal soldiers and other servants of the republic with enormous land grants in California. Two of the northern Channel Islands — Santa Rosa and Santa Cruz — were deeded in this fashion.

Santa Rosa was granted in 1843 to Jose Antonio Carillo and his brother, Carlos Carillo, who established a cattle-ranching operation there. They handed the island over to their daughters in 1844; the women were married to American traders — Alpheus Basil Thompson and John Coffin Jones — who entered into a partnership and managed the ranching operations until 1857, when they sold the island to Thomas Wallace More and Alexander More. Alexander More later bought out his brother, and he was sole owner of the island until his death in 1893.

The island was managed by More's heirs until 1902, when it was purchased by the Vail & Vickers Co., formed by cattle ranchers Walter Vail and J.V. Vickers. The ranch remained in the hands of the Vail and Vickers families until 1987, when the National Park Service purchased it for $30 million and added it to Channel Islands National Park.

The other privately owned island, Santa Cruz, was granted by California Governor Juan Alvarado in 1839 to Andrés Castillero, who owned it until 1857. He sold it to American William Barron, who in 1869 sold it to the Santa Cruz Island Co., incorporated by 10 investors.

In 1880, Justinian Caire became the company's majority stockholder, and under his direction the cattle-ranching operation expanded greatly. The island was too large to manage effectively from a single location, so nine areas were developed as outpost headquarters. Houses, barns, bunk houses, a chapel, a mess hall, a blacksmith shop and a saddle shop were built, with many of the construction materials — particularly bricks and stone —

produced or obtained on the island. Sheep, pigs and horses joined the cattle herds, and in 1884 the ranch expanded into the wine business, constructing a winery and planting vineyards.

Over the next century, the island continued to function as a ranch, with only minor changes — Prohibition ended the winery operation, and sheep became the primary livestock. Through sales, marriages and inheritances, portions of the island passed through the hands of a number of different families. By the 1970s, the island was owned by two families: the Gherinis, descendants of the Caire family, and the Stantons, who had purchased the western nine-tenths of the island from the Santa Cruz Island Co.

Carey Stanton, a Santa Barbara physician, inherited two-thirds of the family's interest, and his nephew, Edwin Stanton III, inherited the other third. Carey Stanton entered into an agreement with The Nature Conservancy — a private, non-profit conservation organization that acquires and manages ecologically significant land — to turn his share over to the Conservancy upon his death; the Conservancy then bought out Edwin Stanton's interest for $1 million.

Dr. Stanton died in 1987, giving the Conservancy ownership of 90 percent of Santa Cruz Island. It restored many of the original ranch buildings, eliminated exotic animal species, and set as its primary mission the preservation of the island's biological, archaeological and historical resources. It manages its holdings as the Santa Cruz Island Preserve, in

Main ranch house, some day to be park visitor center, on Santa Rosa Island

cooperation with the National Park Service.

Members of the Gherini family continued to own the east end of the island; in 1990 and 1992, several members sold their 75 percent share of ownership to the National Park Service. Unhappy with the offered price, Oxnard attorney Francis Gherini retained his 25 percent interest in the 6,500 east-end acres until 1997, when federal legislation forced him to sell it to the Park Service.

San Miguel, Santa Barbara and Anacapa were never deeded to private owners but remained part of the public domain when the United States took possession of Mexico's California territory in 1848, following the Mexican-American War. Americans used them periodically for sheep and cattle grazing as early as the 1850s, and some of the ranchers — squatters, really — treated the islands as their private property even though none of them held legal title.

Anacapa and Santa Barbara islands — small, barren and lacking permanent water sources — were of relatively little interest. West Anacapa was used for sheep grazing from 1869 until the 1930s, when drought and overgrazing finally brought an end to the practice. East Anacapa suffered the same destructive use from 1902 until 1911, when the Coast Guard took it over and built a lighthouse station there in response to several notable shipwrecks. The first "lighthouse" was an unmanned acetylene beacon placed atop a 50-foot metal tower. It was replaced in 1932 by the tower that still stands on the island today. Coast Guard crews were stationed on the island to maintain the beacon until it was automated in 1966; the old buildings now house the Park Service facilities on the island.

Santa Barbara was also used as a ranch and farm from about 1915 into the mid 1920s, but the same problems that rendered Anacapa unsuitable for such a purpose doomed these efforts also. The Navy used the island off and on as an early warning post and to track missiles, before relinquishing control to the Park Service.

San Miguel, although buffeted by strong winds and rough seas, proved far more interesting to ranchers and farmers because of its ample forage and several year-round springs. For some years before 1850, a rancher named Samuel Bruce ran sheep on San Miguel, and he claimed ownership of the island itself, but he sold his interest to former mountain man George Nidever. Nidever stocked the island in 1850 with sheep, hogs, cattle and horses, and profited greatly from the operation until 1864, when drought and overgrazing resulted in the loss of most of his animals and devastation of the island vegetation.

Nidever sold out in 1869 to Hiram Mills, who with his brother put title to the island under the Pacific Wool Growing Co. They built a house on the island but eventually found the life there too harsh and the ranch unprofitable. They sold in 1887 to William Waters, who built a number of structures and expanded the ranch operations. Waters was a bit of an eccentric and would eventually proclaim himself the "king" of San Miguel, believing that the island had never actually been transferred into American ownership after the war with Mexico. The federal government disagreed and reserved the island for a lighthouse in 1909, declaring the private title long claimed by various ranchers to be without legal basis. Waters was allowed to lease the island for $5 a year, which he did until his death in 1917.

San Miguel was then leased to a pair of mainland ranchers, Robert Brooks and J.L. Moore. One of their managers on the island, Herbert Lester, also would later proclaim himself the "king" of San Miguel, and he frequently entertained visitors at the rugged, windswept ranch compound.

The island's ranching days began to draw to a close in 1934, when President Franklin Roosevelt transferred jurisdiction over the island to the Navy. Restrictions on grazing were imposed, and fees increased. When World War II broke out, the island was isolated. Lester, ailing and despondent, eventually killed himself.

The Navy revoked the island lease in 1948, and removed the civilian inhabitants and their property. It then started using the island as a bombing range, eventually closing even the waters around San Miguel to prevent boaters from straying into range of bombs, missiles and live ammunition fired at targets moored near the shore or positioned on the island's peaks. This destructive abuse of the island continued until creation of Channel Islands National Park in 1980, when the island was transferred from Navy jurisdiction to that of the National Park Service.

Channel Islands National Park is still very much a work in progress; the final piece of private island property did not pass into public hands until 1997, and the park staff is still working slowly to develop visitor centers and campgrounds, and to transform livestock trails and dirt ranch roads into hiking paths. So it is somewhat surprising to note that efforts to protect the islands for their stark beauty and unique biological resources began well before World War II.

In 1938, after several years of lobbying by biologists and others who'd come to know the richness of the island ecology, President Franklin Roosevelt created Channel Islands National Monument, which included all of Santa Barbara Island and most of Anacapa, save only the area reserved for the lighthouse. The Park Service requested a survey of San Miguel Island and the regional biologist recommended it be included in the new monument. World War II intervened, however, and the Navy's use of the island as a bombing range took precedence.

Channel Islands National Monument, oddly, was administered by the superintendent of Sequoia National Park, and between 1939 and 1957 no one from the Park Service even visited San Miguel Island. In 1957 monument headquarters moved from Sequoia to Cabrillo National Monument headquarters in San Diego, where at least the trip was shorter. Again, regional Park Service staff began asking their superiors in Washington to press for expansion of the monument.

Influential local voices were added to the clamor in the early 1960s, particularly that of Santa Barbara News-Press publisher Thomas Storke. In 1962 the Navy and the Park Service entered an agreement to cooperatively manage San Miguel Island, and in 1963 California's representatives in Congress introduced the first of several unsuccessful bills that would have upgraded the monument to national park status and expanded it to include all five of the islands.

Monument headquarters moved to Oxnard in 1967, and a new superintendent, William Ehorn, arrived in 1974. Under his direction, monument staff began assessing the islands' biological, archaeological and historical resources, and began developing a management plan. Provisions were made to introduce visitors to Anacapa, Santa Barbara and San Miguel islands, beginning the crucial process of building public support for preservation.

The cause of preservation was taken up in the 1970s by the area's congressman, Robert Lagomarsino, who succeeded where his colleagues had failed. In 1980, President Jimmy Carter signed into law the bill creating Channel Islands National Park, comprising Anacapa, Santa Cruz, Santa Rosa, San Miguel and Santa Barbara islands. The Park Service was authorized to begin negotiations to purchase the private property on the two privately held islands. The same year, the waters within six nautical miles of each island were designated a national marine sanctuary.

Negotiations to acquire the private holdings on Santa Rosa and Santa Cruz dragged on for years. Eventually, most of Santa Cruz ended up in the hands of the Nature Conservancy, which manages it in cooperation with the Park Service. Santa Rosa was purchased in 1987, although the owners were granted a 25-year lease during which they may continue to graze cattle on the island so long as it does not damage the native ecosystem. The final piece of the puzzle was put into place on Feb. 10, 1997, when ownership of the eastern tip of Santa Cruz passed finally to the Park Service.

Plants and Animals

Because they are isolated from each other and from the mainland, each of the Channel Islands has distinctive flora and fauna. Many of the animals and plants found in the park are found nowhere else. Others are similar to their mainland counterparts but have evolved under the pressure of the islands' unusual environments into different forms.

Bird life is abundant. Nearly 200 species visit or reside on the islands, which serve as major rookery sites for cormorants, western gulls, black oystercatchers, Xantus' murrelets, storm-petrels and pigeon guillemots. West Anacapa hosts the largest breeding ground of the endangered brown pelican in the western United States. The larger islands are home to raptors that feed on the population of small rodents: red-tailed hawks, American kestrels and peregrine falcons.

Channel Islands National Park is justly famed for its population of pinnipeds (Latin for "fin-footed"). San Miguel, especially, attracts thousands of seals and sea lions to breed on its remote, protected shoreline, including California sea lions, northern elephant seals, harbor seals and northern fur seals. Rare Guadalupe fur seals and Steller sea lions occasionally haul out on the beaches.

Offshore, the waters teem with fish and other marine life, including some of the most spectacular inhabitants of the Pacific: gray, blue, fin, humpback and killer whales. Pacific white-sided dolphins, common dolphins and porpoises cavort in the swells, and great white sharks prowl the near-shore waters hunting for their favored prey, the seals and sea lions. Forests of giant kelp hide a great diversity of rockfish and other creatures. Altogether, 27 species of cetaceans and 25 species of sharks pass regularly through the park waters.

On land, the islands host relatively few animals. Mice and rats constitute the primary mammalian life; the larger islands also host a unique species of fox. Related to the gray fox of the mainland, the island fox is tiny, only the size of a house cat. It is, nevertheless, the largest land predator in the park, feeding primarily on deer mice. The rare island spotted skunk, an endemic, is found only on Santa Rosa and Santa Cruz.

Non-native animals have also made their mark on the island. Sheep, cattle, horses, rabbits, deer, elk, goats and pigs have at one time or another been introduced onto the islands; because of the damage they inflict on native plant and animal species, the Park Service has adopted a policy calling for these exotics to be eliminated.

Introduced plant species have also left their mark on the islands. Ice

Common dolphin, seen often in the Santa Barbara Channel

**Santa Cruz Island scrub jay,
a distinct species
found nowhere else**

plant, in particular, has overrun vast expanses of Anacapa and Santa Rosa islands. By hogging moisture and leaching salt into the soil, it discourages the growth of native grasses and other plants.

Sixteen plants found on the northern Channel Islands have been proposed for listing as endangered species; many of them are found nowhere else. Altogether, there are 85 plant species endemic to the Channel Islands, ranging in size from the delicate Santa Cruz Island cliff aster to the robust island oak. In some cases, oddity, not rarity, is the distinguishing feature of island vegetation: The giant coreopsis, also known as the tree sunflower, may stand as tall as 10 feet, its feathery golden blooms sprouting from the tips of a bulbous trunk and stems. It looks like a creation of children's author Dr. Seuss, and in springtime the brilliance of its blooms can be seen even from the mainland.

Even odder creatures once inhabited the islands. Fossilized remains of a dwarf species of mammoth have been found on Santa Rosa and San Miguel islands. Paleontologists theorize that their full-sized ancestors swam the 3-mile channel that separated the former island of Santarosae from the mainland during the Pleistocene ice age, and suggest the species subsequently evolved into a pygmy variety in response to the lack of predators and the scant food supply. The island environment was much wetter then, and forests of pine and cypress stood on the mountain slopes. Eerie remnants of the islands' more wooded past are preserved in San Miguel's caliche forests, mineralized tree trunks and roots being exposed as the persistent wind strips away the sand that has long buried them.

Access

There are only two ways to reach Channel Islands National Park: by sea and by air. Visitors aboard private boats may land on Anacapa or Santa Barbara Island without special permission, but a permit from park headquarters is required for landings on Santa Rosa, San Miguel and the east end of Santa Cruz. Landings on west Santa Cruz require a permit from The

Nature Conservancy.

Island Packers, the park concessionaire, offers regular trips throughout the year to all five islands, ranging from half-day sightseeing excursions without landing, to day trips and overnight cruises. They will also transport campers and kayakers with their gear. The company is based at Ventura Harbor next to the park visitor center, but some trips originate at Santa Barbara Harbor and Oxnard Harbor.

Private aircraft are prohibited from flying below 1,000 feet within 1 nautical mile of the islands. Channel Islands Aviation, however, offers flights to Santa Rosa and Santa Cruz islands for passengers planning to hike or camp.

Visitor Centers

Although ranger quarters and displays are located on the islands themselves, the main park visitor center is at Ventura Harbor. It offers interpretive displays, including Chumash artifacts, an indoor tidepool, and a variety of publications, posters and videos. A film and photo exhibits introduce visitors to the island features. The center is open from 8:30 to 4:30 daily, except Thanksgiving and Christmas.

Campgrounds and Lodging

There are Park Service campgrounds on Anacapa, San Miguel, Santa Barbara and Santa Rosa islands, as well as on the east end of Santa Cruz. (The Nature Conservancy allows only day use within the boundaries of its preserve.) There is no fee, but space is limited and permits must be reserved in advance from park headquarters. Only the Santa Cruz campground offers shade, thanks to a grove of eucalyptus trees planted a century ago; on all the other islands, the sites are exposed. Sturdy tents are a must.

Campers must carry all their supplies and gear from the landing to the campground, sometimes up steps and ladders, and sometimes as far as half a mile of steep trail from the landing. All debris must be packed out and removed from the island. Tables and pit toilets are provided, but there are no supplies on the islands. Only Santa Rosa Island's campground has a water supply. Campers elsewhere must bring their own.

In addition to park regulations, the boat operators have restrictions on gear, the most important being a weight limitation of 45 pounds per item. The rule is inflexible; crew members must load and offload passengers' belongings in precarious circumstances, and heavy items would compromise their safety. Complete information about restrictions and requirements is provided with confirmation of boat and camping reservations.

Phone Numbers and Addresses

The park headquarters and visitor center are at 1901 Spinnaker Drive, Ventura, CA 93001. For information and camping reservations, call (805) 658-5730 between 8:30 a.m. and 4:30 p.m..

Island Packers, the park concessionaire for boat travel, is at 1867 Spinnaker Drive, Ventura, CA 93001. For reservations, call (805) 642-1393 between 9 a.m. and 5 p.m. daily. A 24-hour recorded information line may be reached at (805) 642-7688.

Channel Islands Aviation, the park concessionaire for air travel, is at the Camarillo Airport, 305 Durley Ave., Camarillo, CA 93010. It's open from 7:30 a.m. to 6 p.m. seven days a week; for information and reservations call (805) 987-1301.

The Nature Conservancy, which manages the west end of Santa Cruz Island, maintains an office at 213 Stearns Wharf, Santa Barbara, CA 93101. To obtain a landing permit for a private boat, write to the Santa Cruz Island Preserve, P.O. Box 23259, Santa Barbara, CA 93121. Information and reservations for the periodic day trips conducted to the island by the conservancy may be obtained by calling (805) 962-9111. ■

Wind shelters in Water Canyon Campground on Santa Rosa Island

Trails of Anacapa Island

Together, the three small islets that compose Anacapa Island have a surface area of only about 1 square mile, and two of the three — West and Middle Anacapa — are closed to public entry except for one cove and beach open to boaters. The reason for the closure is also the reason Anacapa is worth a visit: wildlife. West Anacapa is the primary West Coast nesting site for the endangered brown pelican, and a host of other birds use the rocky slopes of the middle and east islets to nest and rear their young.

There's only one hike on the island, an easy nature trail that makes a circuit of the flat, rocky surface of East Anacapa. During the nesting season, this trail leads hikers through a scene of rare beauty and spectacle, as thousands of birds stand guard over eggs and chicks, warning intruders away with loud cries and occasional aerial sorties.

Reaching the island is also an adventure. Visitors must book passage on a boat operated by Island Packers, the park concessionaire based at Ventura Harbor, for the 11-mile trip through water teeming with dolphins, sea lions, harbor seals and, between December and March, migrating Pacific gray whales. At the island, the boat backs up against a cliff in the landing cove, holding position on the surging water by gunning its engines, and visitors must grab for a ladder hanging from a platform wedged into the cliff overhead. Once they've scrambled up from the boat's tossing deck, they must climb a steep series of steel and concrete steps to the top of the cliff, some 154 steps in all.

The boat's crew offers plenty of help, but the transfer is still not for the faint of heart or the less-than-agile. It's a thrilling way, however, to begin a visit to a place unlike anything on the mainland. ■

Hike #1: Anacapa Nature Trail

Distance	1.8 miles
Level of difficulty	Easy
Child rating	5 and up
Starting elevation	160 feet
Highest point on trail	200 feet
Topographic map	Channel Islands National Monument
Guidebook map	1

There's no way to get lost on tiny East Anacapa Island even if you should manage to stray from the trail — something park rangers discourage. Because it is the closest to the mainland of any of the Channel Islands, it is easiest to reach. This, combined with its small size, makes it an ideal first trip for anyone hoping to explore the park.

The trailhead is at the visitor center, where there are also picnic tables, restrooms and ranger quarters. The visitor center is a short walk from the platform above the landing cove, where visitors disembark from their boat and climb 154 steps to the top of the island's cliffs. Leaflets offering additional information about the island features are available for 50 cents from a kiosk near the visitor center.

Description

The level trail runs the length of the island from east to west, reaching Pinniped Point at 0.3 mile. The overlook here offers views into Cathedral Cove, where harbor seals and sea lions haul out to bask on the rocky shore. The bulky creatures, so blubbery and awkward as they heave themselves along the ground, become sleek and graceful as soon as they hit the surf.

Past Pinniped Point, the trail passes the small island campground, a barren place with no water or shade. At 0.9 mile the trail crosses a shell midden, an old trash pile left by the Chumash who established seasonal hunting camps here, and reaches the terrace at the west end of the island. From here, the other two islets comprising Anacapa seem almost within reach; separated from each other by narrow channels, they are closed to public entry.

Anacapa is a great block of volcanic rock, and its thin, poor soil supports little. Ice plant is common, although it is an invader originally from South Africa, planted in the 1930s by Coast Guard personnel stationed on the island. Twenty percent of the island's plant varieties are exotic, and they have displaced native vegetation. Some of the rare indigenous species still cling to the island: dudleya, yarrow, gumweed, morning glory and bunchgrass. Giant coreopsis is without doubt the showiest, boasting vivid yellow blooms atop its thick stems in the spring.

The trail loops around to the north, heading back toward the compound. Along the way it passes what appears to be a church; the building is a sham, a shell erected to camouflage and protect the huge, 55,000-gallon redwood water tanks that supply the park staff. The water must be delivered by boat and pumped uphill from the landing cove. Nearby, the trail passes a large concrete slab littered with bird droppings and bones. The slab is a remnant of an ill-fated experiment in water collection, built in the hope that rain draining off its surface could be collected and stored for later use. The plan did not account for the popularity the surface would have with the island's gull population, which found it a perfect place to roost, defecate and gnaw on bits of refuse carried back from landfills on the mainland. Water flowing through such a polluted medium was, to put it mildly, quite unusable.

The trail leads back to the visitor center at 1.8 miles. Beyond, a short spur leads to the Anacapa lighthouse. The first beacon was installed on the island in 1912, following several noteworthy wrecks. Among them was the destruction of the Winfield Scott, a sidewheel steamer that slammed into Anacapa's north shore in dense fog in 1853. The first lighthouse was an unmanned acetylene beacon atop a 50-foot metal tower. In 1932, it was replaced by the current structure, which was staffed by the Coast Guard until 1967, when the beacon was automated. Don't approach the lighthouse; the foghorn is so loud it can permanently damage your hearing.

In addition to the seals and sea lions visible on the shoreline below, Anacapa is a paradise for bird watchers. Seven species of marine birds nest

The "chapel" on Anacapa Island actually conceals redwood water tanks

on the island: western gulls, brown pelicans, double-crested cormorants, Brandt's cormorants, pelagic cormorants, pigeon guillemots and Xantus' murrelets. Bring a pair of binoculars, and fill the time as you wait for the boat back to the mainland by watching their noisy, frantic activity. It's like having your own private Galapagos. ■

Anacapa Island lighthouse

Trails of San Miguel Island

Wild, windswept and lonely, San Miguel is in many ways the most extraordinary of the Channel Islands. Located at the west end of the chain of four northern islands, it lies beyond the protective influence of Point Conception and is exposed to the full force of wind and swells sweeping across thousands of miles of Pacific Ocean. The harsh conditions and its remoteness — 25 miles from the mainland, 50 miles from park headquarters in Ventura — ensure that it sees few visitors. Those who do make the five-hour boat trip must be willing to brave incessant winds, camp under primitive conditions and often endure thick, clinging fog.

The island more than repays this investment. San Miguel suffered the same overgrazing that still mars Santa Rosa and Santa Cruz islands, but it has had more than 40 years to recover, and it now offers a rich and diverse array of native plants. Its beaches are pristine and empty. And for those able to make the long trek to its western tip, it offers one of the great wildlife spectacles of the world: the seal and sea-lion rookery at Point Bennett, where as many as 30,000 animals of six species may congregate at one time on the broad beaches to mate and rear their pups.

Trails also lead to untouched archaeological sites, and rare geological formations. The diminutive island fox strolls frequently through camp on its twilight search for food. Rare peregrine falcons swoop over the broad hillsides on the hunt. Forests of giant kelp sway in the currents just offshore, beckoning snorkelers and scuba divers.

Visitors climb from the boat into a small skiff, which lands through the surf onto the beautiful beach at Cuyler Harbor. From there, it's a long and steep climb up to the top of the bluffs where the trails and the campground are situated. Rough conditions sometimes make it too dangerous to land, so visitors must be willing to accept the chance of disappointment.

Boat trips to San Miguel are generally combined with a side trip to pick up and drop off campers at Santa Rosa Island, which prolongs the journey but offers visitors a chance to enjoy the coastlines of both islands from the sea.

Because of the rare and fragile nature of its treasures, San Miguel has special rules: hikers may not venture away from the campground or the beach at Cuyler Harbor unless accompanied by the island ranger. And as a practical matter, the length of the boat trip and the time it takes to trek to the most interesting sights mean you must plan on camping on the island for at least two nights if you wish to do any real hiking.

But for the hardy and flexible visitor, San Miguel offers a true island experience. In its uncompromising beauty, it is the soul of Channel Islands National Park. ■

Hike #2: Caliche Forest

Distance	3.6 miles
Level of difficulty	Moderate
Child rating	5 and up
Starting elevation	475 feet
Highest point on trail	831 feet
Topographic maps	San Miguel Island East,
	San Miguel Island West 7.5'
Guidebook map	2

Caliche (ka-LEE-chee) is a rock-hard conglomeration of sand and other debris cemented together by calcium carbonate, a mineral common in marine sediments. On San Miguel, the caliche has taken a peculiar form: trees buried eons ago by drifting sand were transformed as percolating water carrying dissolved calcium carbonate faithfully surrounded and replaced their tissues with stone. The sand later blew away, uncovering the stumps and roots of these rocky replicas.

The trail begins at the campground, where there is a pit toilet but no water.

Description

The trail climbs a grassy hillside, reaching the crumbling foundation of the old Lester ranch house at 0.1 mile. The house was built in 1906 of lumber and fixtures salvaged from shipwrecks, and was for many years the headquarters of a sheep-ranching operation on the island. The structure burned many years ago, leaving only the rubble visible today: bits of the main fireplace and chimney, and an underground cistern for storing rainwater.

Just beyond the ruins, the trail crosses a dirt airstrip used by the Park Service to ferry equipment and personnel to the island. The ranger station, visible to the northwest, was designed in imitation of the architecture of the Lester house.

After crossing the runway, the trail climbs through a thick patch of dudleya, a low-growing succulent with gray-green foliage that is endemic to the Channel Islands, surmounts a ridge and descends to a saddle at 0.7 mile, where there are good views to the east across 3-mile-wide San Miguel Passage to the west end of neighboring Santa Rosa Island. The trail resumes its climb and reaches the summit of San Miguel Hill, the highest point on the island, at 1.1 miles. The Navy maintains a small weather station here.

Descending from the 831-foot summit, the trail grows sandy before reaching a junction at 1.7 miles. Bear right, following a spur to the boundary of the Caliche Forest at 1.8 miles.

Caliche forest on San Miguel Island

The forest is cupped by low ridges scoured by the wind. In bright sunlight, the eerie, bone-white stumps cast a striking pattern of shadows across the pale sand surrounding them. Remain behind the barricade, as the caliche is fragile and irreplaceable.

Botanists are not sure what kind of trees served as the model for the stone castings, but pollen studies indicate the island was once wetter and warm enough to support pine and cypress trees, possible candidates for petrifaction.

About a quarter-mile beyond the forest, part way up the side of Green Mountain, lies the wreckage of a B-24 bomber that slammed into the slope in 1943 while searching for a missing Army Air Force plane in dense fog. All aboard were killed, and the wreckage lay there for months before a ranch hand spotted it and reported it to the Navy personnel manning a lookout tower on nearby San Miguel Hill — who somehow had managed to overlook not only the crash and disintegration of the big plane less than a mile away, but the scattered debris as well. That rather astonishing failure offers vivid evidence of how inclement the weather can be on San Miguel.

Through binoculars, it is possible to pick out landing gear and one twisted propeller, as well as bits of unidentifiable debris scattered amid the brush.

Return the way you came.   ■

Hike #3: Harris Point

Distance	6 miles
Level of difficulty	Moderate
Child rating	5 and up
Starting elevation	475 feet
Lowest point on trail	275 feet
Topographic map	San Miguel Island East 7.5′
Guidebook map	2

Harris Point is the northernmost tip of San Miguel Island, a wild, lonely and windswept promontory overlooking a rugged shoreline of rocks, coves and beaches battered by rolling breakers. If you were to sail northwest from the point, the first land you would touch would be the Kamchatka Peninsula, 4,500 miles distant. The winds and waves that rake this spectacular point have traveled uninterrupted over much of the North Pacific.

Spectacular views aren't the only feature of this hike. Because of the harsh conditions, the north side of the island was less damaged by grazing sheep and the native vegetation recovered more quickly there. The route also boasts untouched Chumash archaeological sites, where heaps of abalone and mussel shells rest as if discarded only yesterday — even though they have lain there for hundreds of years — as well as rare caliche castings of plant roots exposed by erosion.

The trail begins, like all the trails on San Miguel, at the island campground. A pit toilet is available, but water is not.

Description

The route backtracks along the trail leading from the beach at Cuyler Harbor up Nidever Canyon to the campground. At 0.26 mile it reaches a junction; turn left, crossing the canyon and passing the former ranger station — a pair of large shipping containers fastened together near a well that has provided water for more than a century. Until 1997, this was where the island ranger lived; the boxes replaced a canvas wall tent, which had in turn replaced a pup tent. The life of the San Miguel Island ranger has always been a bit more demanding than the lives of rangers posted in other parts of the national park system.

Passing the old station, the trail climbs up a ridge and descends into a gully on the other side, reaching the ruins of the original Nidever adobe ranch house at 0.6 mile. All that remains is a pair of wooden beams jutting into a widening gully. George Nidever was a former mountain man, Indian fighter and trapper who moved to Santa Barbara in 1835 to hunt sea otters, married the daughter of a Mexican don and established an extensive sheep ranch on the island in 1850. The adobe dates to that time or perhaps even a little earlier; records are rather hazy.

Beyond the adobe's ruins, the trail climbs to the top of the bluffs at 0.7 mile, where there are terrific views of Cuyler Harbor and its long, white beach. The trail follows the edge of the cliffs for the next mile, crossing a major midden site at 1.7 miles. Abalone shells litter the ground here, along with thick deposits of other shell fragments.

The trail then descends gently into a ravine, passing a scattering of hollow, contorted stone tubes on the right at 2 miles. These are calcium carbonate molds of tree roots, formed as percolating ground water carried the dissolved mineral into the soil and deposited it around the plant material, which then decayed.

From here, the trail undulates as it proceeds the final mile to Harris Point, passing through thick stands of native bush lupine, locoweed, island buckwheat and dudleya before ending in a narrow saddle at the edge of the 200-foot cliff. To the left is Simonton Cove and its long expanse of beach, which faces northwest and catches an interesting array of flotsam carried in by swells traveling across thousands of uninterrupted miles of Pacific Ocean. Below and to the right are the rugged, rocky outlines of Harris Point and Seal Point, along with March Rock and Nifty Rock.

The wind here is fierce and unceasing; the only vegetation clinging to the rocks at the edge of the cliff is a hardy variety of lichen. To stand at trail's end and taste air that last touched land in the Arctic is a remarkable experience, truly one of the best the Channel Islands have to offer.

Return the way you came. ■

Simonton Cove and its beach

Hike #4: Point Bennett

Distance	14 miles
Level of difficulty	Moderate
Child rating	10 and up
Starting elevation	475 feet
Highest point on trail	831 feet
Topographic maps	San Miguel Island East, San Miguel Island West 7.5′
Guidebook map	2

Point Bennett offers one of the great sights of the natural world: the largest West Coast breeding ground of seals and sea lions, and the only place in the world where six species of pinnipeds (Latin for "fin-footed") are known to gather in one spot. In the summer months, it is common for there to be as many as 30,000 animals hauled out on the broad, sandy point at once, a spectacle of noise and motion that nearly defies description. The most common animal is the California sea lion, with northern fur seals running a close second. Other regulars are the northern elephant seal, harbor seal and Steller sea lion, with the very rare Guadalupe fur seal spotted only occasionally.

From a view point at trail's end a quarter-mile from the rookery, the animals may be observed through binoculars and the social structure of their colony appreciated in all its complexity: huge bulls lording it over harems of females and chasing off intruders with roaring charges; small, nimble pups cavorting amid the chaos; thousands of basking adults lying inert on the sand; sleek seals surfing the rolling waves.

The hike is very long — it's 7 miles from the campground to the viewing area — but is over mostly level terrain. It takes a full day, but for those willing to undertake the journey, it offers an unforgettable sight that relatively few people have had the privilege to witness.

The trail begins at the campground, where there is a pit toilet but no water.

Description

For the first 1.7 miles, the trail follows the same route as that described in Hike #2, climbing a grassy hillside, passing the crumbling foundation of the old Lester ranch house and climbing to the summit of San Miguel Hill, the highest point on the island, at 1.1 miles. The Navy maintains a small weather station here.

Descending from the 831-foot summit, the trail grows sandy before reaching a junction at 1.7 miles with the spur to the Caliche Forest. Take the left branch here, dipping into a gully at 2.2 miles and then ascending the flank of Green Mountain, which at 817 feet is the second-highest peak on San Miguel. The trail does not cross its summit, topping out at 2.6 miles and offering views of distant Point Bennett before descending to a level grassland at 3 miles. The trail undulates over the rolling terrain through grasses and hardy shrubs before reaching a dry lake bed at 4.5 miles. A dirt airstrip is maintained here for the use of scientists traveling to the research station operated at Point Bennett by the National Oceanic and Atmospheric Administration. In particularly wet years, the lake may fill. When it does, eggs that have lain dormant in the dry sand for years quickly hatch, and the water is filled with great numbers of fairy shrimp. The shrimp in turn attract great numbers of birds.

The trail continues its gentle undulations, crossing several minor ridges. At 5.5 miles, the sound of barking and bellowing from the thousands of pinnipeds becomes audible even though the point is still out of sight. (Depending on the direction of the prevailing breeze, the smell of all those animals may also become noticeable.) At 5.8 miles the trail tops the final ridge and descends to the NOAA research station at 6 miles.

From the station, the extent of Point Bennett's amazing wildlife spectacle may properly be appreciated. The triangular point has a broad beach protected on the seaward side by kelp forests and a ring of rocks. The point's popularity among pinnipeds is due to a combination of its remoteness, which protects them from human disturbance; the cold ocean current,

California sea lions, northern fur seals and elephant seals at Point Bennett

which supports a rich abundance of fish and squid for food; the offshore kelp, which discourages sharks and attracts bait fish; and the generally foggy conditions, which prevent the seals and sea lions from overheating. They are generally not very adept at regulating their body temperature, and each year many newborn pups die of heat stress before their mothers can get them into the cooling water.

Beyond the research station, the trail drops, steeply at times, a final mile to the dunes at the edge of the beach. Large Chumash middens — thick deposits of shell fragments, bones and other kitchen trash — are visible throughout the dune area. Depending on conditions, the ranger may decide not to allow hikers to approach the dune edge. The animals have a keen sense of smell and are very wary of human beings, and if sufficiently alarmed they may stampede from the beach toward the water, injuring one another and crushing pups to death in their haste.

Be sure to bring binoculars or a spotting scope to derive the most from this opportunity to witness one of the rarest and most awe-inspiring sights of the animal world. When you've had your fill, return the way you came. ■

Trails of Santa Barbara Island

Reaching this southernmost of the islands in Channel Islands National Park is frequently an adventure all its own. The boat ride is long, lasting about four hours, and the few trips scheduled each season by the concessionaire are subject to cancellation because of wind and sea conditions. At the island, if the swells are not too severe, passengers disembark from the boat into a small skiff, which motors across the landing cove to a steel ladder bolted to a wooden landing that clings precariously to the face of a cliff. Hikers must climb from the skiff onto the landing and then climb another quarter-mile of stairs to reach the top of the terrace.

It is worth the effort. Santa Barbara is the smallest of the islands, at about 1 square mile, but it offers a great diversity of animal and plant life. Seals and sea lions swim in the clear waters of the landing cove and congregate by the thousands on the island's rocky beaches. The water is cold but generally clear, and snorkelers enjoy the colorful majesty of the kelp forests, which teem with life. The island is the second-most important seabird nesting site in the park, hosting the world's largest breeding colony of Xantus' murrelets, as well as thousands of western gulls and nesting brown pelicans, an endangered species.

There are about 5.5 miles of trail atop the island, which in topography is basically a big triangular mesa topped by two peaks. The trails lead to overlooks of coves packed with California seas lions, northern elephant seals and harbor seals; skirt rugged volcanic cliffs inhabited by nesting seabirds; and wind among stands of native plants, recovering from decades of abuse by grazing animals.

Campers have plenty of time to roam all the trails. Most day hikers, however, will have to content themselves with one or two, because the length of the boat trip allows only about three hours ashore. In either case, hikers should not rely on the outdated USGS topographic map of the island, but should make sure they have one of the brochures provided by the Park Service. Because of continuing efforts to restore native plants and protect nesting seabirds, trails on Santa Barbara Island are subject to relocation and periodic closures. It's best to consult a ranger before heading out. ■

Hike #5: Arch Point

Distance	2.5 miles
Level of difficulty	Easy
Child rating	10 and up
Starting elevation	160 feet
Highest point on trail	520 feet
Topographic map	Channel Islands National Monument
Guidebook map	3

At the north tip of Santa Barbara Island, Arch Point is the site of a small, automated weather station and a navigation light, and it offers striking views of the east shore with its small-boat anchorage and landing cove. The trailhead is next to the flagpole at the ranger station, at the end of the trail up from the landing cove. There are restrooms but no water.

Description

Proceed west up the hill, bearing left at the first junction at 0.1 mile, and then right at the second junction, at 0.5 mile. Now the trail climbs moderately over the grassy hillside to a four-way intersection in a saddle between Signal and North peaks, at 0.8 mile. Turn right.

The trail climbs the shoulder of North Peak, but does not quite reach the summit before beginning its descent at 1.2 miles. It crosses a grassy hillside, descending moderately to a junction at 1.4 miles with a spur that leads about 50 yards to a bench at an overlook. From the bench are good views of Elephant Seal Cove to the west, where hundreds of California sea lions and northern elephant seals congregate, and Shag Rock to the north, where thousands of seabirds nest.

Beyond the spur, the main trail heads northeast and drops toward Arch Point, crossing the exposed abalone shells and other debris of an unexcavated Chumash midden, or trash heap. Crossing a level plateau littered by worn pebbles of volcanic rock, the trail reaches a junction at 1.7 miles with the spur leading out to Arch Point. Turn left, following the spur to its end next to the light and weather station at 1.9 miles.

After enjoying the view, return to the last junction and turn left, climbing the slope and then contouring through grass and cactus as the trail leads back toward the ranger station. The trail dips into two small gullies along the way, and offers tremendous views of the landing cove and its kelp forests.

Go left at the next junction, at 2.4 miles, returning to the ranger station and your starting point at 2.5 miles. ■

Hike #6: Canyon View Nature Trail

Distance	0.25 mile
Level of difficulty	Easy
Child rating	10 and up
Starting elevation	160 feet
Lowest point on trail	120 feet
Topographic map	Channel Islands National Monument
Guidebook map	3

This very short nature trail serves as a good introduction to the plant life of Santa Barbara Island. It begins at the ranger station and circles the campground, passing signs that identify some of the island's rare, endemic plant species.

Description

From the ranger station, the trail leads south past the restrooms and crosses a grassy hillside covered with stands of giant coreopsis before turning east along the edge of a canyon. The island's volcanic rock, extruded on the sea floor, is pocked with caverns and fissures visible across the canyon.

Passing prickly pear and cholla cactuses, the trail reaches the edge of the bluff at 0.1 mile, offering nice views of the ocean and the island's rugged shoreline. Buckwheat, tarweed and poppies are among the native plant life to be seen along the way.

From the bluff, the trail curves back around to the northwest, passing the ranger station and its large array of solar panels before returning to the starting point at 0.25 mile. ■

Hike #7: Elephant Seal Cove

Distance	3.2 miles
Level of difficulty	Moderate
Child rating	10 and up
Starting elevation	160 feet
Highest point on trail	460 feet
Topographic map	Channel Islands National Monument
Guidebook map	3

San Miguel Island hosts the largest congregation of pinnipeds in Channel Islands National Park, but Santa Barbara boasts a large population of its own, primarily California seal lions and northern elephant seals, which breed and bear young in the protected, rocky coves, and feed on abundant sea life in the kelp forests that ring the island.

This trail leads to a rocky overlook where visitors with binoculars can spend hours watching the antics of hundreds of seals and sea lions surfing the waves, basking in the sun and jostling for position on the rocks. Their raucous barks echo from the cliffs and mingle with the harsh cries of seagulls to form a loud and unforgettable cacophony.

Description

Proceed west up the hill, bearing left at the first junction, at 0.1 mile, and then right at the second junction, at 0.5 mile. Now the trail climbs

California sea lions

moderately over the grassy hillside to a four-way intersection in a saddle between Signal and North peaks, at 0.8 mile. Go straight, descending moderately steeply toward a terrace that reaches back from the edge of the cliffs. The trail levels out at 1.1 miles and skirts the edge of the cliff as it leads northwest toward Webster Point, a lovely scene of crashing surf and rugged cliffs pocked by wave-cut caverns.

The trail turns northeast across the neck of land between Webster Point and the rest of the island, reaching the north shore and descending sharply across loose rocks to an overlook above Elephant Seal Cove at 1.6 miles.

Stay back from the crumbling edge of the cliff, where footing is unsafe. The cove curves away to the east and north, and features a rocky shoreline at the foot of dramatic 200-foot cliffs where hundreds of seals and sea lions gather. A smaller cove to the east is also home to a large number pinnipeds, making the overlook a noisy, fascinating place to pause for lunch.

Return the way you came.   ■

Hike #8: Signal Peak

Distance	3.3 miles
Level of difficulty	Moderate
Child rating	10 and up
Starting elevation	160 feet
Highest point on trail	634 feet
Topographic map	Channel Islands National Monument
Guidebook map	3

Signal Peak is the highest point on Santa Barbara, and the trail to its summit takes in most of the south half of the island. The route skirts the edge of rugged cliffs overlooking Sutil Island, an important seabird rookery a little less than a half-mile offshore, and passes through several nesting grounds of the western gull.

Description

The trail climbs moderately across the grassy hillside overlooking the landing cove to a junction at 0.1 mile. Bear left, winding across the sloping plateau past isolated stands of giant coreopsis, which in spring bears blooms of bright yellow. At a second junction, at 0.5 mile, go left again, heading south through an eroded badlands containing several western-gull rookeries.

The eggs hatch in June, and the remarkably well camouflaged chicks hide in clumps of brush while they mature, watched over by aggressive and

Western gull and chicks during nesting season

attentive parents. Hikers who pass through before the young gulls fledge and leave the nests, usually in late July, should expect to be harassed by protective adult birds, which make low passes overhead while shrieking loud, incessant warnings.

At 1.2 miles, the trail descends to the head of Cat Canyon, which opens to the sea. Exposed rock here is covered with a thick growth of lichen, and stands of cactus and clumps of an endemic species of buckwheat found only on Santa Barbara dot the hillside.

The trail then climbs, nearing the edge of the cliff and offering good views of Sutil Island to the southwest before leveling out at 2 miles. Climbing more gently now, the trail skirts the edge of the cliff, turns inland and reaches the summit, marked by a USGS benchmark, at 2.2 miles.

Beyond the summit, the trail descends gently over a rolling grassland, very different from the rocky, cactus-strewn slopes to the south and east, passes a faint spur on the left, and meets a four-way intersection at 2.5 miles. Go right, descending moderately over the hillside to another junction at 2.8 miles. Continue straight ahead, retracing your steps from here to the trailhead at 3.3 miles.   ■

Trails of Santa Cruz Island

Santa Cruz is almost like a tiny continent, with a richness of plants, animals and topography seldom found on a single island. It has more than 600 species of plants, including nine found nowhere else; more than 260 species of birds, including one — the Santa Cruz Island scrub jay — that has been classified as an endemic species distinct from the mainland jay; and is seasonal host to a wide variety of marine mammals .

Among the island's natural features are metamorphic, igneous and sedimentary rocks, earthquake faults, freshwater streams and springs, mountain ranges that tower 2,400 feet above the sea, coastal beaches and dunes, tidepools, and plant communities ranging from riparian woodland to grassland.

Traveling to Santa Cruz Island is made somewhat complicated by its divided ownership. The National Park Service owns and manages the eastern 10 percent of the island, whereas the western 90 percent of the island is owned by The Nature Conservancy, which calls its acreage the Santa Cruz Island Preserve even though it is technically part of Channel Islands National Park.

Travelers, whether arriving by private boat or on a vessel operated by the park concessionaire, are free to roam wherever they wish on Park Service property. That's not the case on the rest of the island.

The private, non-profit Nature Conservancy acquires and manages ecologically significant land to preserve its natural qualities. Recreation is not one of the organization's priorities, and its management of Santa Cruz Island is no exception. Public access is allowed only when accompanied by a Nature Conservancy guide or with a special permit, which spells out very strict limits on where you can go and what you can do.

Still, it is worth the trouble of arranging passage on one of the guided tours, which may be done by contacting either Island Packers at Ventura Harbor (805-642-1393) or the conservancy's office in Santa Barbara (805-962-9111). The conservancy's naturalists are knowledgeable about the island's unique and fragile resources, and their guidance will enrich the experience for first-time visitors and experienced travelers alike.

Having acquired the last private interest in the property only in 1997, the Park Service is still developing trails, interpretive materials and visitor centers. For now, hikers on park property are pretty much on their own, though rangers are usually on hand to offer guidance, information and advice.

Visitors to East Santa Cruz land on the beach at Scorpion Anchorage or at Smugglers Cove, deposited there by skiff. Hikers bound for The Nature Conservancy preserve on West Santa Cruz climb from the boat onto a pier in Prisoners Harbor. ■

Loading passengers for return trip by skiff and Island Packers boat at Smugglers Cove on Santa Cruz Island

Hike #9: Cavern Point

Distance	2.2 miles
Level of difficulty	Easy
Child rating	5 and up
Starting elevation	10 feet
Highest point on trail	316 feet
Topographic map	Santa Cruz Island D 7.5′
Guidebook map	4

Scorpion Anchorage has long been the place where most visitors have acquired their first taste of sprawling Santa Cruz Island. The location of one of the island's oldest ranch compounds, established in the late 19th century to oversee operations in outlying areas far from the main ranch in the interior, it was for many years the site of a privately run hunting and camping service.

Scorpion is now being transformed into the island visitor center by the National Park Service. Primitive accommodations offered in years past by the private leaseholder near the harbor have been replaced by a 36-space campground, tumble-down sheds have been removed and the century-old adobe ranch house is being remade into a museum and interpretive center.

Set in a grove of eucalyptus trees in Scorpion Canyon, the campground is the most pleasant of any in Channel Islands National Park. Although it lacks water, it has shade and protection from the wind — something not found on the other islands.

The trail to Cavern Point is a short climb from the campground to a bluff offering breathtaking views of the Santa Barbara Channel and the Santa Cruz Island coastline. There are restrooms in the nearby campground, but no water.

Description

The trailhead is at the edge of the rocky beach at Scorpion Anchorage, a small cove that offers tidepools for exploration and good snorkeling amid the kelp that grows in its clear water. Follow the dirt road west up the canyon, passing the ranch compound at 0.2 mile and reaching a junction at 0.3 mile. The trail to the left leads to Smuggler's Cove, and straight ahead lie the campground and the trail to Potato Harbor. Turn right.

The trail leads past a corral and under the drooping branches of several big cypress trees before beginning a moderately steep ascent. After crossing an open, grassy hillside, it follows the course of a small canyon littered with fragments of the volcanic rock that forms the foundation of Santa

Cruz. The dark basalt is covered in many places by layers of pale Monterey shale, which weathers to form a dark, heavy, adobe soil.

At 0.5 mile, the trail crosses the head of the canyon and begins to climb toward a saddle. There are good views to the left of Scorpion Canyon. The trail levels out at 0.9 mile and crosses a plateau of weathered shale before entering a volcanic boulder field and climbing the last few feet to the tip of Cavern Point, at 1.1 miles.

The view from the point is spectacular, encompassing several miles of rocky shoreline and sparkling, blue coves at the foot of 300-foot cliffs. The drop is nearly vertical; if you have children with you, keep them under control.

Return the way you came.   ■

Hike #10: Central Valley

Distance	6 miles
Level of difficulty	Easy
Child rating	10 and up
Starting elevation	10 feet
Highest point on trail	202 feet
Topographic map	Santa Cruz Island B, Santa Cruz Island C 7.5′
Guidebook map	5

The Nature Conservancy uses the historic old ranch headquarters on Santa Cruz Island as employee housing and administrative offices for its management of the western 90 percent of the island. The conservancy acquired ownership in 1987 upon the death of Santa Barbara physician Carey Stanton, whose father had purchased the property in 1937 from descendants of Justinian Caire. Caire purchased an interest in the island in 1869, became sole stockholder in the Santa Cruz Island Co. in 1880, and was responsible for building the ranch into a major producer of beef and wine. The buildings preserved today at the historic headquarters compound in the Central Valley date to his management, and reflect his goal of making the island a self-sustaining colony.

The hike from Prisoners Harbor to the main ranch follows a deep canyon cut by a stream flowing along the Santa Cruz Island fault, and offers visitors the best introduction to the island's rich ranching heritage. The route is nearly level, although it is rocky and requires a few wet stream crossings. Once at the ranch, visitors can see the original ranch buildings — the winery, a chapel, the main house, a bunk house, the shearing shed and others — the oldest of which dates back to 1855.

Some of the buildings serve as private residences and should not be approached out of respect for the privacy of the researchers and Nature Conservancy staff living in them.

The trailhead is at the end of the pier in Prisoners Harbor. There are no restrooms or water available.

Description

From the landing, follow the road southeast from the cove, passing a storage building constructed in 1887 of bricks made on the island. The European-style architecture reflects the heritage of Justinian Caire, who was born in the French Alps, and it is replicated in all the ranch buildings dating from his tenure.

The road forks at 0.2 mile, the left branch leading to Navy installations on the east end of the island. Go right, continuing on the dirt road as it enters the canyon and passing a spur at 0.3 mile that leads to the left. The spur crosses the stream bed and provides access to the well that provides water for the ranch headquarters. Although there are plans to convert the island to solar energy, the pump is powered by a noisy diesel generator.

Just beyond, the road enters a large grove of eucalyptus, an exotic tree planted many years ago on the island to provide shade and serve as a windbreak. The edge of the road is lined with sweet fennel, another invading species, which has spread extensively since sheep were removed from the island. Nature Conservancy biologists have not figured out a way to eradicate the fennel, which is displacing native plants and greatly complicating the task of restoring the island's natural ecosystem.

The canyon also contains many willows and oak trees. The beautiful island oak is an endemic species, found only on Santa Cruz, and illustrates the botanic richness of this largest and most topographically diverse of the Channel Islands. More than 600 species of plants are found here; of the 85 plant varieties found only in the Channel Islands, nine occur only on Santa Cruz.

At 0.6 mile the road/trail enters the rocky river bed on the floor of the canyon, where it will remain until just before it reaches the ranch entrance. Although there is ample evidence of violence in this broad channel — water-tumbled boulders, huge tree trunks and other heavy debris transported from far upstream — the creek flows underground most of the year in this stretch.

The route winds back and forth across the gravelly stream bed. Huge old oaks cling to the craggy canyon wall on the left, while cactus and low-growing shrubs dominate the drier, south-facing slope on the right. The arid appearance of the landscape is deceiving: Santa Cruz receives nearly twice the annual precipitation measured at Ventura on the mainland.

At 1.9 miles the canyon narrows, squeezed by weathered outcrops of 24-million-year-old volcanic rock. At 2 miles, the stream flows above ground, and the trail makes the first of many wet crossings over the next three-quarters of a mile.

At 2.8 miles, the trail climbs above the stream, passes through a fence and reaches a wooden bridge leading to the ranch compound. The road forks at the bridge; the left spur leads a short distance to the picturesque chapel, built in 1891, and the graveyard where members of the Caire and Stanton family lie buried next to a number of ranch employees.

Continue straight ahead, following the road to the main ranch house at 3 miles.

The original two-story adobe house, which has been expanded and remodeled over the years, dates from 1855. Behind it stand the old bunkhouse and the mess hall, built in the 1880s. On the hillside to the left

Chapel and other buildings at main ranch

are a pair of long brick buildings, the lower of which housed the island's winery. Built in 1890, it was the center of a successful operation that produced more than 50,000 gallons a year of zinfandel, chardonnay and other varietals until Prohibition put it out of business.

Other buildings in the compound include the horse barn and tack room, now serving as an auto shop, built in 1888; the milking barn (1888); the sheep-shearing shed (1869); and the slaughterhouse (1890), which, because of its distance from the rest of the buildings, now houses the generator.

A tiny building near the laundry, just down the hill from the main ranch house, has been turned into a museum of Chumash culture by the Santa Cruz Island Foundation, and contains many artifacts.

During Justinian Caire's time, the island was self-sustaining. In addition to cattle, sheep, hogs and wine, the ranch produced olives, apples, pears, quinces and peaches, and a huge garden provided produce. Building materials consisted of brick fired on the island and rubble gathered from the rocky stream beds, saddles and ropes were made by ranch hands, and even the iron for nails, barrel hoops, fencing and other necessities was forged in the island's blacksmith shop.

The grape vines are gone, and only a few head of cattle and a few feral pigs remain of all the thousands of head of livestock that once grazed the hillsides and canyons. Today, the ranch is a quiet relic of a different era.

Return the way you came.　■

Hike #11: Potato Harbor

Distance	4.8 miles
Level of difficulty	Moderate
Child rating	10 and up
Starting elevation	10 feet
Highest point on trail	350 feet
Topographic map	Santa Cruz Island C,
	Santa Cruz Island D 7.5′
Guidebook map	4

This slightly longer trek leads from Scorpion Anchorage on east Santa Cruz Island to an overlook high above one of the island's most picturesque coves. Much of the route lies along a high, wind-swept ridge that offers striking views of the Santa Barbara Channel and a chance to watch the island's abundant bird life — particularly brown pelicans and ravens — play on the brisk updrafts created along the cliff's edge.

The trailhead is at the edge of the rocky beach at Scorpion Anchorage. There are restrooms in the nearby campground, but no water.

Description

Follow the dirt road west up the canyon, passing the ranch compound at 0.2 mile and reaching a junction at 0.3 mile. The trail to the left leads to Smugglers Cove, and to the right is the route to Cavern Point. Straight ahead lie the campground and the trail to Potato Harbor.

The trail is level as it follows Scorpion Canyon west, passing the campground and restrooms at 0.4 mile. Go right at a junction at 0.8 mile and begin climbing the open, grassy hillside above the canyon.

The climb is steady and moderately steep, but the trail levels out at 1.4 miles and contours along the slope. At 1.7 miles it crosses a fenceline and meets the dirt Compo Grande airstrip. After a brief rise, the trail remains flat the rest of the way, making a big curve to the southwest at 2.1 miles and paralleling a fence along the edge of the bluff.

The trail ends on a cliff high above Potato Harbor at 2.4 miles. The harbor gets its name from its shape, irregularly oblong. The water is deep and clear, and supports brown kelp forests. Spectacularly eroded rock formations guard the entrance to the narrow cove, which is popular with snorkelers and divers.

The crumbly shale warrants caution, and the steep drop suggests that parents should keep a close watch on their children.

Return the way you came.   ■

Potato Harbor

Hike #12: San Pedro Point

Distance	7 miles
Level of difficulty	Moderate
Child rating	10 and up
Starting elevation	10 feet
Highest point on trail	650 feet
Topographic map	Santa Cruz Island D 7.5′
Guidebook map	4

San Pedro Point is the easternmost promontory on Santa Cruz Island, and provides awe-inspiring views of the island's coastline, the mainland and the west end of Anacapa Island.

The trail begins at Smugglers Cove, location of one of nine satellite ranches established in the late 1800s to oversee operations in the remote areas of Santa Cruz, which was too large to be administered effectively from the headquarters in the island's Central Valley.

The focus of visitor services and activity on East Santa Cruz is at Scorpion Ranch, where the Park Service is transforming the old ranch house into a visitor center and where the only campground is situated. Commercial boat trips to East Santa Cruz typically end at Scorpion, but on occasion will anchor at Smugglers, depending on weather and sea conditions. When they do, visitors can be assured of a true island experience,

Adobe ranch house at Smugglers Ranch, built in 1889

with an opportunity to visit empty beaches and roam desolate, wind-swept hillsides.

There is no water at the trailhead, and the only restroom is a tiny outhouse intended for use of park rangers who visit Smugglers on patrol.

Description

From the landing beach at Smugglers Cove, follow the dirt road leading to the right as it climbs steeply through an abandoned olive orchard on the hillside above the ranch. At 0.4 mile the climb moderates somewhat, as the trail leaves the orchard and begins crossing the open grassland typical of this part of the island. Years of heavy grazing by sheep all but eliminated the native plant cover, and it will take years for something approximating the natural ecosystem to return.

At 0.6 mile you reach a junction with a faint road that heads straight up the slope to the left. Bear right, remaining on the main road. It reaches one of the island's three air strips at 0.8 mile. This one was popular with bow hunters traveling to Smugglers Ranch to pursue feral sheep, and a decrepit shed near the upper end of the dirt runway bears a whimsical sign announcing it to be the "Santa Cruz Island International Airport."

The road passes the airport "terminal" and heads up the hill behind it, climbing very steeply to the top, at 1.3 miles. The trail then levels out and crosses a fence line at 1.4 miles. Just beyond, a faint set of wheel tracks takes off to the right. Turn and follow them as they head almost due east, passing the head of a canyon and descending gently across a sloping plateau.

At 2.3 miles the trail drops more steeply across a rocky hillside, reaching a junction at 2.4 miles with a faint road leading to the right. Bear left, sticking to the well-defined track as it crosses a low ridge and begins working its way down into a narrow canyon, reaching the bottom at 3 miles and climbing steeply up the other side. The volcanic rock of the canyon wall is pocked with caves, which the island's feral sheep used for shelter.

After climbing out of the canyon, the trail descends moderately across a broad, sloping plateau to the edge of the 100-foot-high bluffs at San Pedro Point, which you reach at 3.5 miles. Straight ahead, West Anacapa Island rises from the waters of 5-mile-wide Anacapa Passage. To the northwest and southwest, the point offers views of the rugged Santa Cruz Island shoreline.

Return the way you came.

Hike #13: Yellowbanks Cove

Distance	4 miles
Level of difficulty	Moderate
Child rating	5 and up
Starting elevation	10 feet
Highest point on trail	500 feet
Topographic map	Santa Cruz Island D 7.5'
Guidebook map	4

Yellowbanks is an anchorage on the east end of Santa Cruz Island. Popular with snorkelers because of its clear water and its kelp beds, it is just southeast of Smugglers Cove, location of the historic Smugglers Ranch.

The trail to Yellowbanks climbs from Smugglers Cove and crosses a ridge offering magnificent views across Anacapa Passage to the west end of Anacapa Island. There is no water at the trailhead, and the only restroom is a tiny outhouse intended for use of park rangers stationed at Scorpion, who visit Smugglers on patrol.

Description

From the landing beach at Smugglers Cove, head inland through the grove of towering eucalyptus that shade some rustic picnic tables. Follow the dirt road up the canyon, passing the adobe ranch house, a windmill and several huge English walnut trees at 0.2 mile. Just beyond the house, the trail drops into the rocky streambed at the bottom of the steep-walled canyon. Crossing to the other side, the trail begins a moderately steep and steady climb at 0.4 mile.

As it climbs, the trail offers good views down onto Smugglers Ranch. The grove of regularly spaced trees on the opposite slope above the adobe is an olive orchard that dates from the ranch's heyday in the last century.

At 0.8 mile the climb grows less steep as the trail reaches the crest of the ridge near a fence line and curves south and then southeast. At 1.1 miles the trail forks. Go left, contouring along the hillside and then beginning a descent across a sloping plateau overlooking the ocean.

At 1.6 miles the descent grows more steep as the trail nears the edge of the bluff. The former ranch road you've been following fades out here, but footpaths lead on down the slope to the south. Scramble down to the first gully on your right, being careful of your footing on the loose, crumbly shale, and follow it down into the canyon, visible directly ahead. Turn left at the bottom of the canyon and hop over the boulders as you follow it to the beach, at 2 miles.

The cove is small and private, with a brown sand beach and a nice view of West Anacapa, making it a fine place for a picnic lunch. When you're ready to relinquish your Robinson Crusoe fantasy, return the way you came. ■

Abandoned olive orchard above Smugglers Cove

Trails of Santa Rosa Island

 Traveling to Santa Rosa Island is like traveling back nearly two centuries, to the time when California was the domain of first Spanish and then Mexican rancheros. The island's 53,000 acres are virtually devoid of human presence, consisting almost entirely of grasslands grazed by thousands of cattle, deer and elk.

None of those three creatures really belongs on the island; all were brought there by those who owned it before the Park Service took over. The persistence of so many non-native herbivores, with the damage they can do to native plants and fragile waterways, is the cause of considerable controversy over the park's management of this second-largest of the Channel Islands. The ranching operation is allowed to continue until 2011 under a special permit issued by the Park Service — among the terms of the purchase — but environmental groups have been pressing the Park Service to substantially limit the ranching operation to protect water quality and endemic species.

For now, hiking on Santa Rosa Island continues to be like hiking through a working ranch, which it is. Cattle and horses roam freely, and the unmistakable traces of their presence degrade the experience considerably. Still, the scenery is remarkable: rugged canyons, long beaches, rolling hillsides, and one of only two groves of Torrey pines in the world. The island is surrounded by kelp beds, supporting a rich array of marine and bird life. Beneath the short, wiry grass that blankets the hills and terraces are hundreds of archaeological sites, mostly ancient trash mounds full of shell fragments.

Whether they travel by air or by sea, visitors land at Bechers Bay on the northeast shore of the island. There are no real hiking trails developed as yet on the island, but the dirt ranch roads offer access to some of the sights within a few miles of the pier and the landing strip. Presumably, this network of roads extends throughout the island, but the Park Service does not offer a decent map, nor are the USGS topographic maps of much use. Most of the island thus remains inaccessible to footbound travelers.

The two trails described in this chapter offer a taste of the island's scenery. Remember that the cattle and horses are skittish and should not be approached. And stay out of the ranch compound itself, just north of the ranger station. Although the island belongs to the public, the ranch is still considered a private inholding. Be prepared, also, for rigorous conditions. It is frequently quite windy on the island, and the sun can be merciless. Conversely, thick fog can roll in and clothe the island in a thick, wet blanket. Bring a hat, wind jacket, water and plenty of sunscreen.

Campers and hikers arriving by boat are put ashore on a pier used by the ranch to load cattle onto boats for shipment to slaughterhouses on the mainland, and their gear is transported through the ranch compound by Park Service truck in order to minimize traffic through the private operation. Those who travel to Santa Rosa by air are deposited on a dirt strip just south of the ranger station and must carry their gear themselves. Park volunteers offer guided truck tours of some of the more remote areas of the island for those who don't want to explore on their own. ∎

Hike #14: Cherry Canyon

Distance	3.6 miles
Level of difficulty	Moderate
Child rating	5 and up
Starting elevation	100 feet
Highest point on trail	650 feet
Topographic map	Santa Rosa Island North 7.5′
Guidebook map	6

Cherry Canyon is one of several steep, rugged canyons carved into the hills of Santa Rosa Island by streams swollen with winter storm runoff. Because it offers moisture and shelter from the incessant winds that sweep across the island, the canyons harbor more diverse plant communities than the exposed ridge tops and hillsides, including groves of oak and wild cherry trees.

This trail leads into Cherry Canyon and then climbs the ridge above it, offering views down into its jumbled topography and out over the landscape of the island's northeast corner. The description follows the trail only as far as a saddle at the head of the canyon, where hikers can look out over San Miguel Passage and see the shore of Santa Rosa's neighbor to the northwest, San Miguel, the outermost of the northern Channel Islands.

The trailhead is at the ranger station, which is roughly midway between the island's dirt runway and the pier. Visitors will have landed at one or the other, unless they have arrived by private boat and anchored off the beach.

There are public restrooms at the ranger station. Water is available at the campground about three-quarters of a mile away, but it's best to bring an adequate supply.

Description

Follow the dirt road west alongside the ranger station, entering the canyon and following the course of the creek. The bluff on your left exposes layers of sedimentary rock, and supports a small stand of giant coreopsis along its top edge.

At 0.3 mile the road forks. Go left, turning into the mouth of the canyon and crossing the stream bed at 0.4 mile. The trail begins a moderately steep ascent at 0.5 mile, climbing the side of the ridge past stands of oak trees.

The canyon below is rugged and eroded into fanciful shapes by running water. The steep slopes support many large shrubs and trees, in contrast to the stubble-clad hillsides above. Sharp-eyed observers may catch a glimpse of some of the mule deer and Roosevelt elk that roam the island, imported to provide sport for hunters.

At 0.9 mile the climb grows less steep as the trail nears the head of the canyon and begins curving toward the south. The trail reaches the saddle at 1.8 miles. Although windblown, it offers a good vantage point to enjoy views of Bechers Bay, Carrington Point at the extreme northeast tip of the island, and the hazy bulk of San Miguel Island to the northwest.

If you're feeling energetic, a longer hike is possible by continuing 1.5 miles beyond the saddle to the top of Black Mountain, the second-highest peak on Santa Rosa, which is visible directly ahead. Otherwise, return the way you came. ■

Hike #15: Torrey Pines

Distance	5.7 miles
Level of difficulty	Moderate
Child rating	10 and up
Starting elevation	100 feet
Highest point on trail	650 feet
Topographic maps	Santa Rosa Island North, Santa Rosa Island East 7.5′
Guidebook map	6

Torrey pines are slow-growing conifers found in only two places: On the coast near Del Mar in San Diego County, where the groves are protected in a state preserve, and on the east end of Santa Rosa Island. The trees seldom grow more than 30 feet tall under the harsh conditions of the island, and generally live no more than 100 years. Their cones, which resemble those of gray pines, contain nuts that are an attractive food source for birds.

This semi-loop trail leads along a flat marine terrace overlooking the offshore kelp beds, climbs atop a ridge with expansive views of the east end of the island, and circles the groves of rare Torrey pines. It serves as an ideal introduction to the landscape of this large island, which is about 15 miles long and 10 miles wide.

The trailhead is at the ranger station, which is roughly midway between the dirt landing strip and the pier. Visitors will have landed at one or the other, unless they have arrived by private boat and anchored off the beach.

There are public restrooms at the ranger station. Water is available at the campground about three-quarters of a mile away, but it's best to bring an adequate supply.

Description

Follow the dirt road south as it parallels the shore, making sure to close and latch the gates you pass through. Remember, Santa Rosa Island is a working cattle ranch; respect its operations and stay clear of the livestock.

There is an intersection at 0.7 mile with a road leading to the right up Water Canyon, where the island's only campground is situated. Continue straight ahead. At 0.8 mile the trail descends steeply into the canyon near its mouth and crosses the creek. After climbing just as steeply out the other side, the trail passes through a gate and forks. Bear left, continuing along the terrace overlooking the beach along Bechers Bay.

At 1 mile you reach the first of the Torrey pines, which are scattered along the hillside above the trail for the next mile. At 2 miles the trail climbs slightly before dropping at 2.2 miles into a ravine. It then turns inland and begins a steep climb. At 2.3 miles, a fainter set of wheel ruts takes off to the right. Follow this track as it climbs steeply up the ridge, heading west toward the island's interior.

At 2.7 miles the trail forks. Stay to the right, crossing the top of the ridge and enjoying terrific views of this part of the island. To the southeast is Skunk Point, with its dunes and beaches, while to the northeast lies the graceful sweep of coastline embracing Bechers Bay. Inland, to the west, are rolling, grass-covered hillsides cut by canyons and gullies. The rugged bulk of Santa Cruz Island looms out of the ocean due east, and the mainland is clearly visible beyond.

At 2.9 miles the trail reaches the Torrey pine grove again. The trail contours along the ridge before climbing to the summit at 3.2 miles. At 3.9 miles the trail leads through a gate; turn right at the junction just beyond and begin descending, steeply at times, toward the terrace, which you reach at 4.7 miles. Pass through two gates, rejoining the road back to the ranger station at 4.8 miles. From here, retrace your steps to the trailhead, which you reach at 5.7 miles. ■

Rare Torrey pine grove, with Bechers Bay in the distance

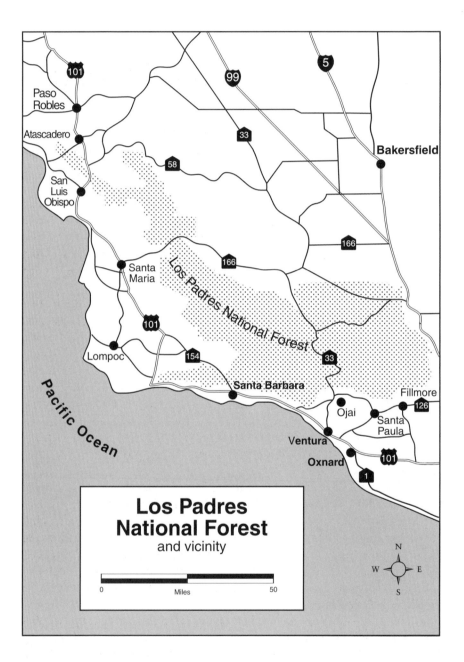

Los Padres
National Forest
and vicinity

0   Miles   50

N
W ◆ E
S

Paso
Robles

Atascadero

San
Luis
Obispo

Santa
Maria

Lompoc

Pacific Ocean

Santa Barbara

Ojai

Ventura

Oxnard

Santa
Paula

Fillmore

Bakersfield

Los Padres National Forest

Los Padres National Forest

Geological History

Sprawling over nearly 1.8 million acres in six counties, Los Padres is the third-largest national forest in California. It encompasses a major portion of the coastal mountain ranges, and consists of two disconnected units. The northern unit lies wholly within Monterey County, outside the scope of this book, and includes Big Sur and the Ventana Wilderness. The much larger southern unit occupies nearly half the acreage in Ventura and Santa Barbara counties, and reaches well into San Luis Obispo County. Its features range from pine-clad mountain peaks to river-cut canyons, chaparral-covered hillsides and arid badlands.

Geologically, the landscape of Los Padres is the meeting point of two major regions in California: the Transverse Ranges and the Coast Ranges.

The Transverse Ranges include the Santa Ynez Mountains of Santa Barbara County and a host of smaller ridges and mountains in Ventura County, including Pine Mountain, the Topatopa Mountains, and the Sierra Madre. There is no single name for this collection of peaks, ridges and hills in Ventura County, a matter of considerable frustration to local travelers. What the mountains all have in common is their peculiar east-west orientation, which they share with the rest of the Transverse Ranges in Southern California: the San Bernardino, San Gabriel, San Jacinto and Santa Monica mountains.

Examination of a map of California offers a clue to the puzzlingly perpendicular orientation of the Transverse Ranges. The coastline makes a great bend at their location. The curve is matched by a corresponding kink in the San Andreas Fault system, which marks the boundary of two moving slabs of Earth's crust, the Pacific Plate and the North American Plate. The Pacific Plate, which lies under the ocean but is also carrying a slice of coastal California on its back, is sliding north relative to the motion of the North American Plate.

Along most of the boundary, the two plates grind past each other in fits and starts, producing earthquakes. But at the bend, the north-moving Pacific Plate has become hung up on the protruding edge of the North American Plate. Instead of sliding past its neighbor, the Pacific Plate is crunching into it. The force of the collision has compressed and crumpled

65

the landscape, creating the Santa Ynez Mountains, the Sierra Madre and the other Transverse Ranges.

The Coast Ranges, on the other hand, behave as a typical mountain range should. They run north-south, parallel to the coast from Santa Barbara County to Oregon. Being more under the influence of the sea, they tend to be moister and cooler than the southern mountains, and they support a different range of plants and animals. Of course, there is considerable overlap; the mixture of plants and animals in the forest is as diverse and complex as its geology.

In broad outline, the mountains that constitute the majority of Los Padres terrain began as sediments gathering for millions of years on the bottom of the sea. Beneath those sediments was ancient bedrock, into which molten rock had intruded and cooled, forming granite. Over time, the motion of Earth's tectonic plates crumpled the landscape of the Transverse Ranges, thrusting the mountains skyward. Erosion carved deep canyons and in some places uncovered the ancient roots of the mountains.

The tallest peaks in the forest — Mt. Pinos, Mt. Abel and Mt. Frazier, in the southeast corner — have outcrops of 2.6 billion-year-old gneiss and schist, metamorphic rocks produced when heat and pressure deformed even older, sedimentary rocks. On Mt. Pinos and Tecuya Mountain, outcrops of granite may be found. Much of the landscape, however, consists of weathered layers of sandstone and shale, uplifted, folded and faulted during the last 10 million years. Streams have cut deep canyons along many of the fault lines.

The Coast Ranges were shoved up in a very different fashion. Long before the San Andreas Fault developed — less than 100 million years ago but more than 30 million years ago — the Pacific Plate dove beneath the North American Plate instead of slipping past it, as the two collided head-on. Parts of the oceanic crust, along with islands and deep-sea sediments, were scraped off on the west edge of the North American Plate, which also was thrust up by the collision. The Coast Ranges are one result of that encounter.

Human History

Los Padres National Forest is the heart of Chumash territory. One of the largest of California's native tribes, the Chumash numbered as many as 30,000, and their occupation of the area dates back 10,000 years. At the time of European contact, they lived in 75 to 100 large villages scattered from Malibu Canyon in the Santa Monica Mountains on the south, to Morro Bay on the north, and inland as far as the western edge of the San Joaquin Valley.

Chumash occupying the mountains and inland valleys within what is now Los Padres National Forest had a way of life distinct from that of Chumash living along the coast and on the Channel Islands. Coastal groups were dependent on the sea for their livelihood, subsisting first on shellfish and later developing the technology and techniques of fishing with nets and hooks, and of taking marine mammals such as seals and seal lions with clubs and spears. Inland Chumash, on the other hand, were much more dependent on acorns collected in the huge oak groves, grass seeds gathered on the extensive grasslands and mountain meadows, and terrestrial mammals such as deer and rabbits taken with snares and stone-tipped projectiles.

The inland villages, however, were not exclusively dependent on terrestrial food sources. The presence of shellfish and marine mammal remains in village trash heaps indicates that the inland Chumash maintained trading networks with their coastal relatives. Many of the roads and trails penetrating the rugged forest today follow those old trade routes.

The forest also preserves rich evidence of Chumash spiritual beliefs, in the form of colorful paintings on cave walls and rock outcrops deep in the mountains.

Europeans established a permanent presence in the region in 1782, when Franciscan missionaries established a mission they called San Buenaventura, near the mouth of the Ventura River at the site of a large Chumash village. Four years later they established another mission at Santa Barbara, followed by La Purísima Concepción, near present-day Lompoc, in 1787, and Santa Ynez, in a mountain valley north of Santa Barbara, in 1804.

Coastal Chumash were the first to succumb to the mission influence, and the rugged mountains proved only a temporary haven for those living in the interior. Within 50 years, disease and social disruption at the hands of the military and religious authorities had decimated the Chumash population and all but destroyed its culture.

The mission system itself ended shortly after Mexico's independence from Spain in 1822. The vast lands held by the missions were turned over to private owners, and huge tracts of promising territory were granted to war veterans and other favored individuals. Most of the rugged Los Padres region remained untouched, but huge ranches were established in the valleys with good streams and rivers: Santa Ynez, Ojai, Sisquoc, Cuyama, Sespe.

Americans acquired much of the land following Mexico's defeat in the Mexican-American War, and during the Gold Rush period of the late 1840s and early 1850s prospectors scoured the canyons of the Los Padres region looking for precious minerals. They found little, although remnants of their activities may still be found along Piru and Lockwood creeks, where modern-day gold seekers still sift the gravel bars looking for wealth.

Many of the prospectors stayed on to become farmers, settling in the canyons and the large meadows high in the mountains. In the 1880s, a faith healer named Hiram Wheat founded a religious commune in the remote Sisquoc Valley. Faint remnants of these settlements may still be found in some of the lonely valleys, where ruined cabins and long-abandoned fruit orchards testify to the pioneer spirit.

Efforts to preserve the forest, not for its timber but because of its importance as a watershed for the growing communities along the coast, began in the late 1800s. President William McKinley created the forerunner of the Los Padres in 1889, when he withdrew more than 1 million acres of the public lands in the mountains to form the Zaca Lake and Pine Mountain forest reserves. In 1908, President Theodore Roosevelt withdrew more acreage and combined it with the earlier reserves to form the Santa Barbara National Forest. After additional expansions, the forest was renamed Los Padres in 1938 in memory of the Franciscan priests who founded the missions.

Evidence of the forest's importance as a source of water for lowland communities is provided by the 19 reservoirs within or near its boundaries: Lake Cachuma is a primary source of water for western Ventura County; Lake Casitas serves a similar purpose in Santa Barbara County. The city of Santa Barbara also maintains several dams and reservoirs in the Santa Ynez River drainage, including Gibralter Reservoir and Jameson Lake. Twitchell Reservoir on the Cuyama River in San Luis Obispo County is a major source of water in the Santa Maria area.

Los Padres is one of the most roadless forests in the country, fully 90 percent of it classified as untouched. Aside from some mineral exploration and dam construction, there has been little incentive to pave it. In recognition of its pristine character, the forest contains 10 national wilderness areas, comprising 813,366 acres — 46 percent of its total area. It also has 1,542 miles of trails and 84 miles of Wild and Scenic Rivers.

Paradoxically, Los Padres is also one of the most urban of national forests. Because the front country is within easy driving distance of much of Southern California's growing population, the 10 percent of the forest that is cut by roads incurs heavy use. According to the Forest Service, it logs more than 14 million visitors per year. Many of those travelers merely drive through the forest on scenic highways, stopping only to picnic or admire the view, but an increasing number take the time to hike or camp.

In recognition of this heavy burden, Los Padres in 1997 became one of four national forests in the country to charge a day-use fee of $5 per car, under an experimental program authorized by Congress. (The other three are the most heavily used urban forests in the country: the Angeles, San

Bernardino and Cleveland, all on the edge of the Los Angeles urban area.) The money is supposed to be used in the national forest where it is collected, and only for recreation programs, such as trail repair and construction, campground maintenance and interpretive activities.

Only time will tell whether the public is prepared to pay for an activity that has always been free, even if it would reverse years of deterioration.

Plants and Animals

The forest offers great diversity in its ecosystems: riparian corridors, grassland, arid badlands, pine-clad mountain peaks. Along its rivers are thick stands of oaks, sycamores and cottonwoods, while the cooler, moister slopes harbor Coulter pine, gray pine, big-cone Douglas fir, white fir and ponderosa pine. In some areas, the pinyon-juniper habitat — more common in the high desert country — may be found in conjunction with the sagebrush community characteristic of the Great Basin.

The predominant vegetation is chaparral, accounting for 68 percent of the national forest acreage. It comprises dense, woody shrubs tolerant of heat and drought and adapted to periodic wildfire. Chamise, toyon, laurel sumac, sage, scrub oak, manzanita and ceanothus cover most of the slopes, along with yucca and several varieties of cactus — proof of the stingy rainfall. Fire is a great and persistent threat in Los Padres National Forest, and although the native plant communities require its cleansing passage to clear out decadent growth and return nutrients to the soil, it is fought nearly everywhere it occurs.

The forest is home to hundreds of species of birds, including golden and bald eagles, peregrine falcons and six species of hawks, as well as a wide variety of mammals. Black bears, coyotes and mountain lions are common, as are wild boars, mule deer, blacktail deer and many species of rodents.

The forest's most famous inhabitant is the California condor, the largest and rarest bird in North America. Although it once ranged over nearly the entire United States, the population of condors dwindled steadily as people moved west. By the end of the 19th century the huge vultures could be found only in Southern California, where they inhabited a wishbone-shaped territory encompassing the Coast Ranges south of Monterey, the Sierra Nevada south of Sequoia National Park, and portions of the Transverse Ranges. Los Padres National Forest was the heart of this last stronghold.

Even in this rugged terrain, and even with their food supply augmented by the hundreds of thousands of cattle and sheep being grazed in the hills and valleys bordering their range, condors continued to dwindle because of shooting, theft of their eggs and lead poisoning — the result of condors ingesting lead shot in animal carcasses and gut piles left by hunters. Biologists estimate their number at around 600 as the 20th century dawned; by the time the first organized field observation was launched in 1939, the condor population had dwindled to as few as 60. Even creation of two condor sanctuaries within Los Padres — the Sespe and Sisquoc — did nothing to halt the slide.

The condors' numbers fell to only 22 individuals in 1982. A captive-breeding program was established, and the remaining wild condors were captured and placed in zoos in the hope their numbers would rebound and the species could one day be returned to the wild.

The program has so far succeeded. By early 1997, there were more than 130 California condors, most of them hatched and reared in captivity, and biologists have released several groups into the wild. Two of the primary release sites are in Los Padres National Forest, the last stronghold of the birds, and hikers on Pine Mountain and in the Sierra Madre have a fair chance of seeing one of the huge scavengers float by on wings that stretch nearly 10 feet from tip to tip.

Access

The forest is within easy reach of several cities strung out along the major north-south freeway on the California coast, U.S. Highway 101. Ventura, Santa Barbara and San Luis Obispo are the largest of these. State highways penetrate the forest in several places; those of greatest interest to hikers are Highway 33 in Ventura County and Highway 154 in Santa Barbara County. Interstate 5 skirts the east side of the forest, providing access to the backcountry for travelers northbound from Los Angeles.

The best overall map for those planning a visit is the Los Padres National Forest map published by the Forest Service, available at good outdoor shops and Forest Service offices.

Visitor Centers

Los Padres National Forest has no real visitor centers, but information, maps and a few publications are available at the forest headquarters in Goleta and at district ranger headquarters in Ojai, Frazier Park, King City, Santa Barbara and Santa Maria. They are open weekdays from 8 A.M. to 4:30 P.M.

Campgrounds

There are 97 forest campgrounds reachable by car, and scores more that have been developed along trails at popular sites in the backcountry. For visitors planning to hike the Los Padres trails described in this book, nine of the car camps are of particular interest.

Cerro Alto: 8.7 miles southwest of Atascadero on Highway 41. Elevation 1000 feet. 26 sites. Open year-round. Fee $16 a night. Water, tables, fireplaces and pit toilets. *(Hike #16.)*

Figueroa: 13 miles from Los Olivos on Figueroa Mountain Road. Elevation 3500 feet. 32 sites. Open year-round. No fee. Tables, fireplaces and pit toilets provided. *(Hike #19.)*

Juncal: 20 miles east of Santa Barbara via East Camino Cielo and Juncal roads. Elevation 1800 feet. 6 sites. Open year-round. No fee. Tables, pit toilets and fireplaces but no water. *(Hikes #18, 20, 22.)*

Lion: 6 miles east of Highway 33 at the end of Rose Valley Road. Elevation 3000 feet. 30 sites. May be closed in winter. No fee. Tables, fireplaces and pit toilets but no water. *(Hikes #29, 31.)*

Pine Mountain: 4.5 miles east of Highway 33 on Pine Mountain Road. Elevation 6700 feet. 8 sites. May be closed in winter. No fee. Tables, fireplaces and pit toilets, but no water. *(Hike #28.)*

Reyes Peak: 5 miles east of Highway 33 on Pine Mountain Road. Elevation 6800 feet. 7 sites. May be closed in winter. No fee. Tables, fireplaces and pit toilets, but no water. *(Hike #28.)*

Rose Valley: 4 miles east of Highway 33 on Rose Valley Road. Elevation 3400 feet. 9 sites. Open year-round. No fee. Tables, fireplaces and pit toilets, but no water. *(Hikes #29, 31.)*

Sage Hill: 6 miles east of Highway 154 on Paradise Road. Elevation 1100 feet. 62 sites. Open year-round. Fee $8. Tables, fireplaces, flush toilets and water. *(Hike #17.)*

Wheeler Gorge: On Highway 33, 9 miles north of Ojai. Elevation 1750 feet. 68 sites. Open year-round. Fee $15 a night. Water, tables, fireplaces and flush toilets. *(Hike #32.)*

Except for Wheeler Gorge, all these campgrounds are available on a first-come, first-served basis. Reservations for Wheeler may be made by calling (800) 280-CAMP.

Although most of the campgrounds require no overnight fee, campers should be aware that the Forest Service requires visitors to purchase a day-use pass to park nearly anywhere in Los Padres — including at "free" campgrounds. The only exceptions are those areas where a specific use fee is already collected for camping or parking. The pass comes in two versions: a $5 daily pass and a $30 annual pass. They are available at all ranger stations, as well as local stores and gas stations. Contact forest headquarters for an updated list of local outlets.

Failure to display the pass in your vehicle while parked at a trailhead in the forest can result in a $100 fine.

Food, Gas and Lodging

Full services are available in the communities adjacent to the forest, particularly Ojai, Ventura, Santa Barbara, Los Olivos, Santa Maria, San Luis Obispo and Atascadero.

Phone Numbers and Addresses

For general information about Los Padres National Forest, write to headquarters at 6144 Calle Real, Goleta, CA 93117, or call (805) 683-6711. For more specific information regarding trail and campground conditions, contact the appropriate district office.

Santa Barbara Ranger District: Star Route, Santa Barbara, CA 93105; (805) 967-3481.

Mt. Pinos Ranger District: Star Route, Box 400, Frazier Park, CA 93225; (805) 245-3731.

Ojai Ranger District: 1190 East Ojai Avenue, Ojai, CA 93023; (805) 646-4348.

Santa Lucia Ranger District: 1616 Carlotti Drive, Santa Maria, CA 93454; (805) 925-9538.   ∎

Trails of
Los Padres National Forest

From the ocean to the mountains, Los Padres National Forest offers a broad range of hiking experiences, and the trips selected for this guide sample all of them. By picking and choosing, hikers should also be able to find trips for every season, a matter of some importance in the Los Padres, where winter brings snow to the mountains and summer bakes the lowlands in unbearable heat.

The trips are grouped by county, and most are in the part of the forest near the cities of Santa Barbara and Ventura. Both communities serve as good bases from which to explore the forest.

Because so many of the hikes originate at trailheads near urban areas, getting started often requires navigating local streets and roads, and the trail maps included in this guide do not lend themselves to detailed depiction of these. Before setting out, it is a good idea to obtain a street map of each community, such as those published by the Automobile Club of Southern California.

Remember also that starting in mid-1997, Los Padres became one of four national forests in Southern California to adopt a pilot day-use fee program. Intended to generate sufficient money to provide trail and campground maintenance not possible under current budget constraints, the pass costs $5 a day or $30 for a full year and must be displayed on any car parked in the forest. The only exceptions are those parked in areas where a fee is already collected, such as campgrounds and some parking lots. Failure to display the permit can result in a $100 fine. ∎

San Luis Obispo County

Hike #16: Cerro Alto

Distance	5 miles
Level of difficulty	Moderate
Child rating	10 and up
Starting elevation	1000 feet
Highest point on trail	2624 feet
Topographic map	Atascadero 7.5′
Guidebook map	7

In translation, Cerro Alto means simply "high hill," a rather unimaginative name for this delightful peak in the northern Los Padres National Forest. Fortunately, the views from the summit are much more inspiring than the name, encompassing a great expanse of the central coast from Morro Bay inland to the Salinas River valley and the distant bulk of the Temblor Range.

The trail begins at Cerro Alto campground, which is off Highway 41 about halfway between Highway 1 in Morro Bay and Highway 101 in Atascadero. The turnoff to the campground, 7.3 miles east of Morro Bay and 8.7 miles west of Atascadero, is on the south side of the road and is clearly marked.

Drive through the campground and park in the dirt lot next to the ranger's cabin. The campground is a pleasant one, strung out along the banks of tree-shaded East Fork Morro Creek. The overnight fee is rather steep, $16, perhaps because this campground is managed by a private concession company under a contract with the Forest Service. That's more expensive than a spot in Yosemite Valley, and Cerro Alto doesn't have flush toilets, showers or any of the other amenities that make people willing to pay so much.

The trail begins at a sign next to site #19. Water and restrooms are nearby.

Description

The broad, well-maintained trail climbs moderately in the shade of oaks and California laurels, following the creek up the canyon. The creek supports a lush growth of plants and an abundance of songbirds, and for the first 0.5 mile hikers stay close to the water.

Beyond the first half-mile, the trail crosses the creek and climbs up the side of the canyon, steeply at times, until it is high above the creek.

Evidence of past wildfires is preserved in the form of charred stumps and snags on the hillside, which is thickly covered with drought-tolerant chaparral.

At 1 mile the trail intersects an old dirt road. Turn right, following it uphill about 50 yards, and then bear left as the trail leaves the old road. The trail rejoins the road at 1.2 miles, as good views of the mountains to the west and east begin to open up. The rocky trail ascends steadily and lacks shade from here on, although the glare of unbroken sunshine is compensated for by the wealth of flowers lining the trail, among them bush monkey flower, pearly everlasting, bush poppy, morning glory and hummingbird sage.

At 1.7 miles the trail grows level and begins contouring along the side of Cerro Alto. At 1.8 miles a sign marks a junction with the trail to the summit, which leaves the dirt road and goes to the left. The climb is steep for the next half mile, bringing terrific views of Morro Bay and the Pacific Ocean at 2.3 miles. At 2.4 miles is a junction; go left, ascending steeply and reaching another junction, with an old road, at 2.7 miles. Go left again, and climb to the volcanic outcrops of the summit at 3 miles.

After enjoying the spectacular 360-degree view, retrace your steps through the first two trail junctions, watching your footing on the loose, treacherous rock, and return to the sign at the dirt road at 4.2 miles. Instead of continuing back the way you came, go left, following the dirt road downhill to a junction at 4.3 miles with a trail that drops steeply to the right into a canyon that leads back toward East Fork Morro Creek.

Poison oak abounds along this section of trail, which crosses an open hillside and then passes through a nice grove of oak trees, unscarred by fire, at 4.8 miles. The trail drops again and crosses a footbridge over the creek in the bottom of the canyon at 4.9 miles. The trail then climbs up to the campground road, emerging next to site #16. Follow the road back to the parking area, at 5 miles. ■

Santa Barbara County

Hike #17: Aliso Canyon

Distance	3.5 miles
Level of difficulty	Moderate
Child rating	10 and up
Starting elevation	980 feet
Highest point on trail	1740 feet
Topographic map	San Marcos Pass 7.5'
Guidebook map	8

The trail offers hikers two options: The first mile consists of a signed interpretive trail keyed to an informative brochure geared toward children, offering a fine introduction to the natural history and the Native American adaptations to the region. It follows an easy course along a small stream and is suitable for even young children. Older hikers, however, may enjoy continuing beyond the end of the interpretive trail to complete the full 3.5-mile semi-loop hike, which leads to the top of a ridge above Aliso Canyon and offers fine views of the Santa Ynez River valley and surrounding mountains.

The trailhead is at the Sage Hill Campground in the Santa Ynez River Recreation Area. To reach it, take Highway 154, the San Marcos Pass Road, from Highway 101 in Santa Barbara and follow it 11 miles to Paradise Road. Turn right and follow this paved, two-lane road 4.5 miles to the Los Prietos Ranger station. Turn left at the ranger station and follow the narrow road across the Santa Ynez River to the signed campground entrance. Turn right when the road divides just inside the entrance and proceed to the day-use parking area at the east end of the campground.

Water and restrooms are nearby. There is a $3 day-use fee. The trail begins on the north side of the parking area next to a large sign. A box on the sign contains free trail leaflets.

Description

Following the course of Aliso Creek, which is dry in its lower reaches by early summer, the trail is broad and well-maintained, thanks to the efforts of the Los Padres Interpretive Association. The route is shaded by large coast live oaks and sycamores growing along the stream banks; the hillsides above are covered with a thick growth of chaparral.

The trail crosses the stream bed at 0.1 mile and then recrosses it a few yards upstream. At 0.3 mile you reach a junction; continue straight along the canyon, crossing the creek again about 40 yards further. There's usually water at this crossing, even in late season. There are numerous crossings beyond this point, as the trail winds back and forth along the canyon floor.

At 0.6 mile the trail climbs briefly, leaving the stream and crossing a hillside covered with sage. At 0.7 mile the trail begins to descend, offering good views of the upper canyon, and reaches the canyon bottom again at 0.9 mile. About 50 yards beyond, you reach a junction. Bear left, crossing the stream a final time and reaching the end of the interpretive trail on a flat under a large oak tree at 1 mile.

If you have young children with you, stop here and retrace your steps from this point. To complete the full Aliso loop, walk back over the stream and turn left at the junction, beginning a moderately steep ascent of the canyon wall. The views are very good back down toward the mouth of Aliso Canyon, but the trail is quite exposed and is best hiked early in the day. Yucca and sagebrush cover the rocky slope.

At 1.3 miles the trail begins following a small canyon as it curves east away from Aliso Canyon, leading to the lower edge of a broad meadow at 1.6 miles. The Santa Ynez Mountains are dotted by many of these odd grass-covered gaps in the predominant chaparral, gaps known by the Spanish term *potrero*.

The trail reaches a saddle on the ridge between Aliso Canyon and Oso Canyon at 1.7 miles. The trail forks here; turn right, following the trail along the spine of the ridge. Sage and chamise form a uniform wall of tall vegetation on the slopes.

At 2.2 miles the trail begins climbing down from the ridge, curving to the west and offering terrific views of the Santa Ynez River nearly 1000 feet below. The trail crosses another potrero, ringed by oak trees, at 2.8 miles, and then begins a switchbacking descent into Aliso Canyon. The trail rejoins the interpretive trail at the floor of the canyon at 3.2 miles. Turn left and follow it back to the parking area at 3.5 miles. ∎

Hike #18: Blue Canyon

Distance	3.2 miles
Level of difficulty	Easy
Child rating	5 and up
Starting elevation	2100 feet
Lowest point on trail	1925 feet
Topographic map	Carpinteria 7.5′
Guidebook map	9

Blue Canyon gets its name from the outcrops of serpentine, a mottled, blue-green rock, found along its walls. Formed through the metamorphosis of magnesium- and silicate-based rocks deep beneath the sea floor, generally in the presence of ocean water and tremendous heat, serpentine has a distinctively greasy or soapy feel to it.

This trail follows the course of a small creek past scenic rock formations deep within the Santa Ynez mountains, to a small backcountry camp near a series of inviting pools and small cascades.

To reach the trailhead, take the Mission Street exit from Highway 101 in Santa Barbara and head north toward the Santa Barbara Mission, turning left on Olive Avenue and then right on Mission Canyon Road. Just past the Mission, turn right onto Mountain Drive and follow it to Gibraltar Road. Turn left and follow Gibraltar Road 7 miles as it climbs high into the mountains, and then turn right onto East Camino Cielo, at a sign indicating the route to Pendola Station. Drive east 7 miles to Romero Saddle, where the road becomes rough dirt, but suitable for most passenger cars. Continue on the dirt road, bearing left at a fork, 4 more miles to the trailhead, which is on the left just after you cross a bridge.

Park in the pullout. A sign indicates the start of Trail 26W12. No restrooms or water are available.

Description

The trail is rocky, and begins dropping immediately toward the bottom of Blue Canyon, following the course of the unnamed creek. Oaks and sycamores offer sporadic shade as the route levels out and passes through chamise chaparral.

At 0.3 mile the trail passes a colorful outcrop of weathered sandstone, stained red and yellow. You begin a gentle descent, passing a mineral spring at 0.4 mile and entering a shady grove of big oak trees. At 0.6 mile you pass an extensive exposure of sandstone, carved into fantastic shapes by erosion.

Dropping to the canyon floor, the trail enters a stand of tall sycamore trees and then crosses the creek at 1 mile. Beyond the crossing, the route is shaded by dense growth of oaks and alders. You climb above the creek a bit and pass an outcrop of serpentine at 1.1 miles, before descending to cross a small tributary stream at 1.3 miles.

After dropping steeply, the trail crosses another small creek at 1.5 miles. Upper Blue Canyon Camp is on a small bench just above the water. Continuing past the camp, you reach the bank of the main creek at 1.6 miles. This is a good stopping place, deeply shaded and featuring many pools suitable for wading, splashing, chasing minnows and catching polliwogs.

Return the way you came.   ∎

Hike #19: Davy Brown Trail

Distance	6 miles
Level of difficulty	Strenuous
Child rating	10 and up
Starting elevation	3780 feet
Lowest point on trail	2100 feet
Topographic map	Figueroa Mountain., Bald Mountain 7.5′
Guidebook map	10

Figueroa Mountain, where this hike begins, is on the edge of the San Rafael Wilderness. It offers a variety of attractions throughout the year: spectacular wildflower displays in spring, a dusting of snow in the winter, and the shade of tall big-cone firs and ponderosa, Jeffrey, gray and Coulter pines when summer heat envelops the lowlands. Year-round streams water its canyons, which are thick with blue oaks, sycamores and big-leaf maples.

The Davy Brown Trail follows one of these canyons, appropriately named Fir Canyon, as it descends steeply from Figueroa Mountain Road to the Davy Brown Campground. The hike down is pleasant, following the course of a lovely little creek, and makes a fine one-way trek for young hikers if a car shuttle is arranged from the campground. Otherwise, the slog back uphill is too strenuous for anyone but the very energetic. Along the way, the trail passes an old mine tunnel and the remains of a cabin built in the 1920s by a chromium miner.

To reach the trailhead, take Highway 154 north from Highway 101 in Santa Barbara and follow it over San Marcos Pass to Los Olivos. Turn right onto narrow, twisting Figueroa Mountain Road and follow it 14 miles, passing a ranger station and then Figueroa Mountain Campground. The trailhead is at a pullout on the left side of the road 1 mile past the campground entrance, just before the road reaches a tall hill of blue-green serpentine.

There are restrooms but no water at the campground nearby. There are no services at the trailhead itself.

Description

The trail climbs over a low ridge next to the road, offering good views back toward the Santa Ynez Valley, before descending moderately past oaks and tall big-cone firs into the Fir Canyon drainage.

The trail clings to the edge of the steep, narrow canyon, crossing the stream bed at 0.5 mile. Just beyond, the creek tumbles over worn bedrock in the shade of bay trees and meets a small tributary stream. The trail turns left across the stream and continues downhill on a more moderate grade, passing beneath large maple trees.

At 0.9 mile the trail reaches a junction. To the left a few yards ahead, a plaque

Humboldt lily is common along shaded streams

mounted on a boulder commemorates the efforts of Edgar B. Davison, the forest ranger who built the Davy Brown Trail in 1898-1899. One of the first rangers in the area, he patrolled what was then known as the Zaca Lake Forest Reserve to protect the trees from illegal cutting and to prevent overgrazing.

Cross the creek and turn downstream, remaining in the canyon bottom. The trail quickly crosses the stream twice more, and reaches the cabin site at 1.4 miles. All that remains are the rock foundation and a scattering of debris. If you backtrack about 100 yards and look carefully across the stream, you will spot the entrance to a mine tunnel dug into the canyon wall.

Beyond the cabin site, the trail and the stream drop more steeply. The pools and cascades are particularly picturesque in this part of the canyon, inviting you to linger in the shade. Enjoy it while you can, for at 1.7 miles the trail leaves the riparian forest and crosses a hot, open hillside burned by a 1993 wildfire. Toyon, bush poppy and other woody shrubs have sprouted up to fill the gaps left by destruction of the mature trees.

At 2 miles the trail returns to the bottom of the canyon and the shade. Winding past several large outcrops of eroded sandstone, the trail grows even more steep, crossing the stream at 2.3 miles and reaching an unmarked junction. Stay to the right, continuing down the canyon and crossing the stream again at 2.5 miles. After two more stream crossings, the trail reaches a broad, oak-studded flat at 2.9 miles and then passes through a gate at the lower end of Davy Brown Campground.

Continue through the gate into the campground, at 3 miles. Named after William Brown, a recluse who occupied a cabin here from 1879 to 1895 after a long and colorful life on the California frontier, the campground on the shady bank of the creek makes a nice place to pause for lunch and — if you have not arranged a car shuttle — to prepare for the tiring return trip back up the canyon to the trailhead.   ■

Hike #20: Forbush Flat

Distance	3.4 miles
Level of difficulty	Easy
Child rating	5 and up
Starting elevation	3425 feet
Lowest point on trail	2350 feet
Topographic map	Santa Barbara 7.5′
Guidebook map	9

Reaching the Cold Springs Saddle trailhead, where this hike begins, is almost as much of an adventure as the hike itself. It requires a long drive on a narrow road that climbs to the summit of the mountain wall looming over the Santa Barbara plain. From the crest of the Santa Ynez Mountains, which the road follows for many miles, the views are breathtaking — the best available from any road in Santa Barbara County. Along the way, you will pass rock climbers testing their skills on sheer sandstone outcrops, and hang gliders leaping into space from atop La Cumbre Peak, to drift and soar over the city before landing miles away on a quiet stretch of beach.

The goal of this hike, Forbush Flat, is tucked into a canyon on the north side of the range. It is named after Fred Forbush, who built a cabin there in 1910 by the edge of a small creek, and planted an orchard of apple and pear trees. The cabin is long gone but some of the trees remain and still bear fruit, a bonus for hikers who reach the meadow in the right season. Forbush Flat also contains a small backcountry camp, with two sites.

To reach the trailhead, take the Mission Street exit from Highway 101 in Santa Barbara and head north toward the Santa Barbara Mission, turning left on Olive Avenue and then right on Mission Canyon Road. Just past the Mission, turn right onto Mountain Drive and follow it to Gibraltar Road. Go straight across the intersection (Mountain Drive goes to the right) and follow Gibraltar Road as it climbs high into the mountains. Turn right after 7 miles onto East Camino Cielo, at a sign indicating the route to Pendola Station. Drive east 4 miles to Cold Springs Saddle and park in the broad turnout next to the concrete water tank. The trail begins across the road, next to a metal sign identifying it as the Cold Spring Trail. There are no restrooms or water.

Description

The trail descends moderately across a shaly hillside covered with scrub oak, toyon, laurel sumac and squaw bush. You climb briefly over debris from a rock slide and then resume the descent, crossing a small creekbed at 0.5 mile. Sycamores and oak trees shade this moist area, which also supports a healthy stand of poison oak.

Beyond the glade your trail contours along the slope, offering good views into the drainage of the Santa Ynez River to the north before growing rocky and resuming its descent at 0.7 mile. The trail drops steadily and the view remains expansive as the trail heads for the bottom of Forbush Canyon, which it reaches at 1.4 miles.

At 1.5 miles the trail splits. The right fork heads east into Forbush Canyon. Bear left, reaching the campground 50 yards farther. The camp, near a small but pretty creek, is shaded by huge oak trees and has two picnic tables and two fire pits. The fruit trees are along the edge of the meadow. The trail leads past them and crosses the flat, reaching the other side at 1.7 miles

The beds of sedimentary rock in the area contain fossil shell deposits, and they reward exploration. After a suitable time enjoying the peaceful atmosphere of this old homestead, return the way you came. Unfortunately, the return route is all uphill. ∎

Hike #21: Gaviota Peak

Distance	6 miles
Level of difficulty	Strenuous
Child rating	10 and up
Starting elevation	600 feet
Highest point on trail	2458 feet
Topographic map	Solvang 7.5′
Guidebook map	11

Although the hike to the summit is long and can be quite hot on a sunny day, Gaviota Peak provides one of the best views available of the northern Santa Barbara County coast, and is more than worth the effort. On a clear day, the panorama can stretch from Santa Barbara to Morro Bay, encompassing about 100 miles of coastline. As a bonus, the trail leads past a local landmark: Gaviota Hot Springs, a series of tepid, sulfur-laden pools popular with bathers.

To reach the trailhead, take the Highway 1-Lompoc exit from Highway 101, 31 miles north of Santa Barbara. Turn east (crossing the freeway if you were southbound), and then turn right on the frontage road. Follow it about a quarter-mile south to the Gaviota State Park entrance. The road dead-ends in a dirt parking lot. There is a $2 fee to park. A portable toilet is provided but no water. The trail begins at the east end of the lot, next to a sign offering information about the trail and warnings about the usual hazards of travel in the coastal mountains: ticks, rattlesnakes, poison oak and mountain lions.

Description

The trail climbs moderately from the parking area, through an oak and sycamore woodland. The first 0.4 mile, up to the junction with a spur leading to the hot springs, is heavily used. Turn left at this signed junction, soon leaving the shade, dropping past a spring and beginning a rather steep climb across an open hillside covered with tall grass, coyote brush and black mustard.

At 0.7 mile the trail re-enters oak woodland. It continues to climb, switchbacking up the hill, and crosses the National Forest boundary at 1.5 miles. The oak woodland is soon replaced by typical chaparral vegetation, including a dense growth of woody shrubs such as chamise and manzanita. At 2 miles the trail reaches a saddle with nice views of the ocean to the west and the valleys to the east.

At 2.3 miles the climb becomes quite steep and rocky. At 2.7 miles the trail crosses an old fence line, and at 2.8 miles it passes a heavy steel gate and reaches a junction at another saddle. The views improve still more, including the ocean and several of the Channel Islands. Thanks to the disorienting trend of the coastline in this area, the islands lie due south as you look out to sea — not west, as you might guess.

Turn right, beginning a very steep climb up a gravelly slope that offers unstable footing. The summit is close, however, and you reach it at 3 miles. There's a cylindrical can at the top containing notebooks in which other hikers have written their thoughts and observations.

The view, like the climb, is breathtaking. After enjoying it for awhile, return the way you came. If your feet are sore, take a quick side trip to the hot springs for a soothing soak.   ■

Hike #22: Montecito Peak

Distance	3 miles
Level of difficulty	Moderate
Child rating	10 and up
Starting elevation	3425 feet
Lowest point on trail	2600 feet
Topographic map	Santa Barbara 7.5′
Guidebook map	9

Montecito Peak juts up from the Santa Barbara foothills, standing apart from the steep wall of the Santa Ynez Mountains like a conical battlement. Because of its position, it offers a slightly different view than the mountain crest, one that reaches all the way to the Santa Monica Mountains. It looks almost directly down on the streets and homes of Montecito and downtown Santa Barbara, including the harbor and beaches. Except for the very steep scramble the final half-mile to the summit, it's an easy walk.

The trailhead is at Cold Springs Saddle, the same as for Hike #17 to Forbush Flat. Take the Mission Street exit from Highway 101 in Santa Barbara and head north toward the Santa Barbara Mission, turning left on Olive Avenue and then right on Mission Canyon Road. Just past the Mission, turn right onto Mountain Drive and follow it to Gibraltar Road. Follow Gibraltar Road as it climbs high into the mountains, and turn right after 7 miles onto East Camino Cielo, at a sign indicating the route to Pendola Station. Drive east 4 miles to Cold Springs Saddle and park in the broad turnout next to the concrete water tank. The trail begins near the tank, next to a metal sign identifying it as the Cold Spring Trail. There are no restrooms or water.

Description

The trail drops moderately across a sunny slope that grows hot by midday. The chaparral is very tall and thick, eventually arching over the trail to form a tunnel of thorny vegetation. However, the path is broad here, so the tough shrubs pose no obstacle, and the shade they provide is quite pleasant.

At 0.6 mile the trail levels out somewhat and contours along the hillside, soon leaving the shade behind. The descent resumes at 0.8 mile, but only for a short distance. At 1 mile the trail levels out again. Look here for the faint spur leading to the left up the rocky slope toward the summit.

The going has been easy up to this point, but beyond here hikers earn the view. The trail is very steep and covered with loose rock, making the footing treacherous. Be careful and take your time, following the trail as it circles around the summit and makes the final approach from the south.

The path reaches the bald crown of Montecito Peak at 1.5 miles. There is a coffee can containing a notebook where other travelers have recorded their thoughts.

The view reaches to the Santa Monica Mountains on the east, and encompasses all the communities of the Santa Barbara coastal region: Carpinteria, Summerland, Montecito, Santa Barbara and Goleta. To the south rises the bulk of Santa Cruz Island, seemingly adrift in the sea haze. With binoculars, you can examine the activity far below on the wide beaches of Santa Barbara.

Montecito Peak, with its clear view of the ocean to the west, would be a great place to watch the sunset were it not for the tricky footing of the descent. If you plan such an outing, be sure to bring a flashlight and don't tarry long after twilight sets in.

Return the way you came, taking care to move slowly down the steep slope below the summit. ■

Hike #23: Rattlesnake Canyon

Distance	3.4 miles
Level of difficulty	Moderate
Child rating	10 and up
Starting elevation	900 feet
Highest point on trail	1950 feet
Topographic map	Santa Barbara 7.5′
Guidebook map	12

Technically, this delightful hike up a tree-shaded canyon watered by a year-round creek is not in Los Padres National Forest, but in a narrow strip of city-owned parkland jutting into the forest. The distinction is purely a legal one, however, for the canyon offers the same enjoyable hiking experience regardless of which agency administers it.

Despite its name, Rattlesnake Canyon has no more of the venomous reptiles than any other area, and it has long been popular with local hikers. The Santa Barbara Chamber of Commerce began purchasing recreation easements from canyon landowners in the early 1900s to maintain public access, and in the 1960s the city of Santa Barbara purchased the land outright and added it to nearby Skofield Park.

Use of the canyon by the local community actually dates back further than that: Hidden along the creek are the remains of a small dam and aqueduct built in the early 1800s to serve the nearby mission.

To reach the trailhead, take the Mission Street exit from Highway 101 in Santa Barbara and head north, following the signs to the Santa Barbara Mission. Drive past the mission to Foothill Road. Turn right, go about a quarter mile and then turn left onto Mission Canyon Road. Follow it about half a mile to its intersection with Las Canoas Road. Turn right on Las Canoas and follow it to Skofield Park. The trail begins on the left side of the road, right before the ornate stone bridge.

Limited parking is available on the shoulder by the bridge, but it's easier and safer to drive on into Skofield Park, leave your car in the lot there and walk the 100 yards back down the road to the bridge and the trailhead. The park also offers water and restrooms. The trailhead is marked by a nice wooden sign proclaiming this to be the "Skofield Park Rattlesnake Canyon Wilderness Area."

Description

The trail crosses the creek and climbs up to an old buggy road, used by the Santa Barbara gentry on their turn-of-the-century outings, then follows its route upstream. At 0.4 mile it crosses an outcrop of Coldwater sand-stone, blocks of which were carved from a nearby quarry to build the estates of neighboring Montecito, and descends to the creek at 0.5 mile. Along the route, many side trails lead to pools and cascades.

After crossing the creek, you climb steeply and pass a grove of Aleppo pines, planted in the mid-1960s by the local Sierra Club chapter to replace trees that had been destroyed during a wildfire. The original grove of pines had been planted in the 1930s by Hobart Skofield, whose father had purchased most of the land in the canyon.

Beyond the grove, the trail climbs rather steeply across an open, sunny slope. At 0.8 mile, good views open up toward the city below. The prominent building on the ridge in the foreground is the Mt. Calvary Monastery. The monastery buildings originally were intended to be a villa, built by millionaire Ray Skofield, who began work on his mountain retreat in the 1920s after buying hundreds of acres in the canyon. His dreams were thwarted, however, by the onset of the Depression.

At 0.9 miles the trail drops. Ahead, the bulk of La Cumbre Peak rises high above the head of the canyon. At 1 mile, the trail is shaded by large canyon oaks, and at 1.1 miles you resume your climb, crossing a gully and then crossing the creek at 1.2 miles.

The trail crosses the creek again at 1.3 miles in the deep shade of large oak and bay trees. The creek forms a series of pools and cascades here, especially inviting if the day is warm.

At 1.6 miles you reach the lower end of Tin Can Meadow, site of a turn-of-the-century homesteader's shack built of flattened 5-gallon kerosene cans nailed to a wooden frame. The shack was long a local landmark, but burned in a wild-fire in the 1920s. At the upper end of the meadow, at 1.7 miles, the trail forks. The right branch offers adventurous hik-ers a steep route up to Gibralter Road and panoramic views of the city. To the left is a con-nection with the Tunnel Trail

Trail maintenance tools for volunteers

in nearby Mission Canyon, location of Hike #24.

The junction is shaded by a huge oak tree, making this a fine stopping place for a snack. As a bonus, the meadow offers a good vantage point to watch hang gliders riding the thermals from the popular launching point on La Cumbre Peak.

After enjoying the quiet and the sight of so many brightly colored aircraft drifting overhead like enormous nylon butterflies, return the way you came.   ■

Hike #24: Seven Falls

Distance	2 miles
Level of difficulty	Easy
Child rating	5 and up
Starting elevation	1000 feet
Highest point on trail	1350 feet
Topographic map	Santa Barbara 7.5′
Guidebook map	12

This easy stroll to a series of rock-rimmed pools on a creek in Mission Canyon is among the most popular short hikes in the Santa Barbara area, particularly in spring and early summer when temperatures are beginning to climb but before the stream level falls too far and the water grows warm and algae-clogged. If you have youngsters, it's a good introduction to the pleasures of hiking: a brief spell of huffing and puffing, rewarded by a cool dip in a natural wading pool.

To reach the trailhead, take the Mission Street exit from Highway 101 in Santa Barbara and follow the signs north to the Santa Barbara Mission. From the mission, follow Mission Canyon Road to Foothill Road and turn right. Turn left a few hundred yards later to rejoin Mission Canyon Road, and follow it to the Tunnel Road turnoff. Go left on Tunnel Road and follow it to the end. Parking is prohibited along the last stretch of this dead-end road. Park on the shoulder, being careful not to block any of the private driveways.

Walk up the road to the locked gate, where the hike begins. No water or restrooms are available.

Description

Follow the pavement as it climbs, steeply at times, through oak trees and chaparral into Mission Canyon. The road was built around the turn of the century during construction of a tunnel that delivers drinking water to the city from its Gibralter Reservoir on the other side of the Santa Ynez Mountains.

The road offers great views almost immediately, back down into Santa Barbara and beyond to the coast and the Channel Islands. At 0.4 mile the road forks; bear left, continuing uphill. At 0.5 mile it crosses a bridge across Mission Creek, just downstream from the portal of the water tunnel. At 0.6 mile the pavement ends and the trail forks just beyond. Stay to the left, continuing to climb and passing an intersection with the Tunnel Trail to the right at 0.7 mile. Continue straight ahead on the narrowing footpath, About

100 yards beyond, the trail forks again. Again, stay to the left.

At 0.8 mile the trail descends toward Mission Creek, which it reaches at 0.9 mile. Cross the creek and turn right, braving the poison oak along the informal trail or boulder-hopping along the creek — a more enjoyable route — to the series of pools and cascades just upstream. The scenery grows more attractive the farther you go, until the route is blocked by a high waterfall at 1 mile. Rock-climbing skills are needed to go beyond this point, as the creek slips and slides through a narrow canyon eroded through slick sandstone.

The pools harbor tadpoles, California newts and tiny fish. Keep a careful eye out for the abundant poison oak, and enjoy the music of the tumbling water.

Return the way you came.   ■

**Pools and cascades
at Seven Falls**

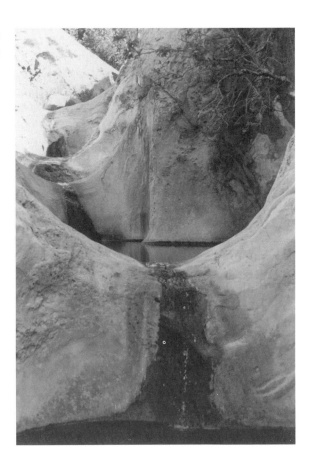

Ventura County

Hike #25: Horn Canyon

Distance	5.8 miles
Level of difficulty	Strenuous
Child rating	10 and up
Starting elevation	1520 feet
Highest point on trail	3260 feet
Topographic map	Ojai 7.5'
Guidebook map	13

Slicing into the flank of Chief Mountain and watered by a small creek, Horn Canyon climbs steeply from the east end of Ojai Valley. The trail leads through creekside willows and cottonwoods, and then switchbacks up a steep slope choked with thorny chaparral before arriving at a delightful picnic spot: a flat high above the valley, shaded by a grove of large Coulter and gray pines.

The trailhead is on the grounds of Thacher School. Follow Highway 150 east from Ojai 1.5 miles to Reeves Road. Turn left and follow Reeves Road 1 mile to McAndrew Road. Turn left and follow McAndrew to the school entrance, at the corner of McAndrew and Thacher roads. Turn right onto the campus and bear right at the fork just inside the entrance, following the signs to the gymkhana field. The road soon turns to dirt and crosses a dry creekbed in an avocado orchard. Just beyond, a locked gate on the left marks the start of the trail. Park in the pullout near the gate. No water or restrooms are available.

Dense brush obscures some stretches of the trail. It is best to hike it early in the spring, when temperatures are still cool enough for long pants to be comfortable.

Description

Walk through the gate and follow the trail north past a sign indicating the start of Trail 22W08 to The Pines Camp. The trail leads across a flat covered with laurel sumac, sage, Spanish broom and mustard. At 0.2 a trail branches off to the left and leads back onto the campus of the private school. Continue straight ahead, entering a woodland of oaks and black walnuts as you climb gently uphill.

At 0.4 mile the trail crosses the creekbed and then continues more steeply up a rocky slope. It recrosses the creek at 0.5 mile, soon passing through a grove of huge oak trees. The climb continues, growing gradually more steep as the trail crosses the stream again at 0.9 mile, passes a well with an electric pump on top, and then leaves the shade to cross a dry, open slope.

The trail dips briefly at 1.1 miles to cross the creek again in a grove of oaks and cottonwoods, shading several nice pools. Beyond, the climb begins in earnest, as the trail leads steeply up the sage-covered ridge above Horn Canyon. After several switchbacks, the trail offers good views back across the canyon to the Ojai and Upper Ojai valleys. The blue gem of Lake Casitas, a major reservoir for this part of Ventura County, lies in the distance to the west.

Continue the steep, steady climb, pressing through a tall stand of chamise over the last half-mile and reaching the shady site of The Pines at 2.9 miles. There are several fire pits here and a hitching post. The Coulter pines are particularly interesting; they bear huge, wickedly knobby cones nearly the size, shape and heft of pineapples. Needless to say, it isn't a good idea to stretch out for a nap beneath one of them.

Return the way you came.   ■

Hike #26: Matilija Canyon

Distance	4 miles
Level of difficulty	Easy
Child rating	5 and up
Starting elevation	1520 feet
Highest point on trail	1700 feet
Topographic map	Old Man Mountain 7.5′
Guidebook map	14

If you are seeking an outing for children, this is the best hike in the Ventura County region of Los Padres National Forest. The trail is well maintained and almost level, and leads up a shaded canyon along the course of a beautiful little creek just the right size for wading and for skipping stones.

To reach the trailhead, follow Highway 33 north from the 101 Freeway in Ventura, through the town of Ojai, following the signs toward Maricopa. Eighteen miles from 101, turn left on Matilija Canyon Road and follow it 5 miles to a dirt parking area near the gate at the entrance to the private Matilija Canyon Ranch. Park here and continue on foot. No water or restrooms are available.

Description

Follow the paved road through the ranch, making sure not to stray from the Forest Service easement onto private property. The road soon turns to dirt and then crosses Matilija Creek at 0.5 mile. This may involve wading if the water is high, but most of the year it requires nothing more than boulder hopping. The road crosses a tributary of Matilija Creek at 0.8 miles. About 100 yards beyond the crossing, a sign marks the start of the trail on the right side of the road.

The trail leads across the rocky bed of Matilija Creek, turns and then crosses North Fork Matilija Creek. Sage, yucca and manzanita carpet the sunny flats, but the trail soon leads into the shade of sycamores and oaks along the creek. At 1.2 miles is a sign marking the boundary of Matilija Wilderness.

Beyond the sign the trail climbs over an old rockslide and returns to the bank of the creek, following it north and crossing again at 1.6 miles. The trail then follows a nearly level course to Matilija Camp at 2 miles.

Located on an oak-shaded flat surrounded by huge boulders, the camp features several fire pits and is conveniently close to the water. The canyon is narrow here, and steep walls of layered sandstone tower above the creek as it tumbles through several nice pools suitable for a cooling dip. There is a fair amount of poison oak in the area, so be sure your children know how to avoid it before you let them ramble unattended.

Return the way you came.   ■

Hike #27: Nordhoff Peak

Distance	11.2 miles
Level of difficulty	Strenuous
Child rating	10 and up
Starting elevation	1160 feet
Highest point on trail	4485 feet
Topographic maps	Ojai, Lion Canyon 7.5′
Guidebook map	15

It is a bit longer than most of the trails in this book, but the well-maintained route to the top of Nordhoff Peak is one of the best in the southern Los Padres National Forest. The grade is steady but never excessively steep, and the view from the summit is jaw-dropping. It's important to pick an appropriate season for this hike, however, as the peak wears a mantle of snow during the winter and the trail can be dry and quite hot between late spring and early fall. Best times are early spring and late fall.

In happy coincidence, these are also the seasons most likely to provide fog-free days — ideal for enjoying the peak's expansive view of the verdant Ojai Valley, the Channel Islands and the rugged interior wilderness.

Nordhoff Peak is named for journalist Charles Nordhoff, who visited the area in 1872 and was so taken with it that he published a series of glowing articles in national publications — including the popular Harper's Magazine — extolling its virtues. As a result, wealthy easterners flocked to the region, establishing a town they named after him. Residents later renamed the community Ojai, a Chumash word meaning "nest."

To reach the trailhead, go north on Highway 33 from Highway 101 in Ventura, driving 14.7 miles to the picturesque little town of Ojai. In Ojai, turn onto Highway 150, follow it east about 2 miles and turn left on Gridley Road, just past the Los Padres National Forest ranger station. Follow Gridley Road north 1.5 miles until it dead-ends at a private driveway. Park on the shoulder, making sure not to block the gate. The trail begins on the north side of the turnaround next to a sign.

Description

The dusty trail is open to mountain bikes and horses as well as hikers, so be alert and step aside if you encounter them. It leads gently uphill through dense brush and trees, following the course of a seasonal creek. Sage, laurel sumac, sycamores and oaks crowd the trail and provide shade.

At 0.4 miles the trail meets a dirt road near avocado orchards on a private ranch. Turn right on this road, continuing uphill and crossing a ranch access road at 0.7 mile. Immediately beyond, the trail forks off to the left and skirts the orchard as it heads toward the edge of Gridley Canyon. The trail grows rocky at 1.2 miles, as the sound of water flowing at the bottom of the steep canyon to the east becomes audible. The slope here is covered primarily by chamise, sage and manzanita, extremely tolerant of heat and aridity. The trail rounds a corner at 1.6 miles, offering a glimpse of the fire lookout atop Nordhoff Peak directly ahead.

At 1.9 miles you cross a trickle of water seeping from a spring, which supports a shady grove of oak trees and moisture-loving ferns. At 2 miles you reach Gridley Spring trail camp, which consists of a steel water tank, a rock fire ring, a hitching post and a makeshift bench. The camp was burned over by the 1985 Wheeler Fire.

The trail grows steeper at 2.7 miles and begins switchbacking out of the canyon. It crosses the outflow from another small spring at 3.5 miles and climbs past a small grove of big-cone Douglas firs onto the crest of a ridge at 4 miles. Beyond, the climb is less steep as the trail works its way around the flank of the peak to a dirt road in a saddle at 4.6 miles.

The view is spectacular already, reaching from the rugged contours of Pine Mountain on the north to the ocean on the south, but will get even better as you turn left and follow the road steeply toward the summit. At 5.5 miles the road forks; turn right, following the spur to the fire lookout at 5.6 miles.

The living quarters atop the lookout have been dismantled, and only the steel framework remains. The view is stunning, including several of the Channel Islands, the patchwork of orchards in the Ojai Valley and Upper Ojai Valley with Sulfur Mountain rising above them on the south, and reaching into the rugged fastness of the Sespe Condor Sanctuary to the east. Pine Mountain looms over the slender stripe of Highway 33 as it climbs through the hillsides northwest of your vantage point, and the rugged Santa Ynez Mountains stretch away to the west.

After a suitable pause to enjoy the sights, return the way you came. ■

**Matilija poppies
beside the trail**

Hike #28: Pine Mountain

Distance	2.2 miles
Level of difficulty	Easy
Child rating	5 and up
Starting elevation	7200 feet
Lowest point on trail	7000 feet
Topographic map	Reyes Peak 7.5′
Guidebook map	16

Snow-covered in winter, a cool oasis of mountain air and evergreen shade in the summer, Pine Mountain offers a touch of the Sierra Nevada in the generally arid and brush-carpeted Ventura County backcountry. Best of all, the daunting climb to the summit can be completed by car, following a narrow road hacked into the mountain's rugged flanks.

The mountain is actually a long, massive ridge topped by several peaks. From road's end, near the highest of these peaks, all routes lead downhill — a backpacker's dream. The summit also offers extraordinary views of the heart of Los Padres National Forest, a harsh and empty wilderness of deep canyons, crumpled badlands and waterless mountain slopes.

Pine Mountain is also California condor country. The primary release site for these endangered birds, which are being bred in captivity and then set free in small numbers in an effort to save them from extinction, is only a few miles away in the Sierra Madre. It is not uncommon for one of the great soaring birds, which have a wingspan approaching 10 feet, to cruise over Pine Mountain while searching for carrion.

This hike is really just a ramble down a fire road that follows the crest of the mountain. It is a perfect outing for a family with tykes, particularly if you are spending the night at one of the small, primitive campgrounds operated by the Forest Service near the summit. It also makes a good leg-stretcher if you've driven up the mountain just for the day to picnic and hope for a glimpse of one of the rarest birds in the world as it cruises in silent splendor on the rising thermals.

To reach the trailhead, drive north on Highway 33 from the 101 Freeway in Ventura, following this slow mountain road 45 miles to the sign indicating the turnoff to the Pine Mountain Recreation Area. Turn right and follow the paved road up the mountain. The road is extremely narrow and has many blind curves, so take it slowly. Although rough in spots, it is passable by standard passenger cars.

At 6.1 miles, the pavement ends at a large gate that is sometimes locked. Park here. There is no water on Pine Mountain, but there are pit toilets back at the Reyes Peak campground.

Description

Hike past the gate and follow the dirt road as it descends gently along the sloping crest of the mountain. The air is filled with the scent of pine, thanks to the abundance of conifers shading the summit: ponderosa pines, white firs, sugar pines and Jeffrey pines.

The view encompasses hundreds of square miles of wilderness. To your right is the deep gorge carved by Sespe Creek. Ahead and slightly to the left is the distant bulk of Mt. Pinos, at 8831 feet the highest peak in the Los Padres. Below on your left is the Cuyama Valley, where patches of bright green irrigated forage contrast startlingly with the arid and apparently lifeless surroundings.

At 1.1 miles the road ends at the boundary of Sespe Wilderness. A trail continues past the berm that marks the end of the four-wheel-drive route, leading to Haddock Peak and points beyond, but the saddle here in the shadow of 7510-foot Reyes Peak makes a fine spot to stop and enjoy the view.

Return the way you came.   ■

Hike #29: Rose Valley Falls

Distance	0.6 mile
Level of difficulty	Easy
Child rating	3 and up
Starting elevation	3425 feet
Highest point on trail	3600 feet
Topographic map	Lion Canyon 7.5′
Guidebook map	17

This easy stroll leads to the most spectacular waterfall in Southern California, a 300-foot cascade that drops in two stages down a sheer cliff not far from a popular campground. Gentle and short enough for hikers of all ages and levels of physical condition, the trail is enormously popular with local residents on hot spring days.

To reach the trailhead, follow Highway 33 north from Ventura 28 miles to the Rose Valley Road turnoff. Go right and follow Rose Valley Road 3 miles to an intersection just before the Rose Valley Work Camp. Turn right and follow the rutted road a short distance to the campground. Park in or near the campground, making sure not to block any of the sites. The trail begins next to site #4. There are restrooms but no water.

Description

About 50 yards from the trailhead the trail crosses a tiny creek, following a thickly wooded canyon gently uphill. The broad, heavily used trail is shaded by huge sycamores and oak trees as it enters the canyon and follows the course of the main creek uphill to the base of the waterfall at 0.3 mile.

**Rose Valley Falls
in summer**

The trail ends in a shaded grotto filled with ferns and mosses. The lower fall is about 100 feet high, and the water splashes and drips in a thousand rivulets across the slick, flower-bedecked cliff.

A faint trail leads across the crumbling slope to the upper fall, but it is unstable and dangerous. Each year, someone is seriously hurt or killed tumbling off the rocks near the waterfall, and it is far more prudent to enjoy the spectacle from a comfortable seat on one of the many boulders scattered about the grotto.

Return the way you came.   ■

Hike #30: Santa Paula Canyon

Distance	6.2 miles
Level of difficulty	Easy
Child rating	5 and up
Starting elevation	1140 feet
Highest point on trail	1720 feet
Topographic map	Santa Paula Peak 7.5′
Guidebook map	18

This popular trail offers one of the area's most pleasant outings, especially for youngsters. Although there is some elevation gain, it follows a generally level course along the tree-shaded route of perennial East Fork Santa Paula Creek, which tumbles from pool to pool through boulders perfect for climbing. The trail climbs to a small backcountry camp in a grove of pines and then descends to a picturesque waterfall that empties into a deep hole great for swimming.

Because it involves climbing over loose rocks on a steep slope, the leg of the hike beyond the camp may not be suitable for young children, but youngsters over 10 should have no difficulty with it.

On warm weekends, the trail is likely to be crowded with local residents seeking relief from the heat in the creek's many pools. An early start is recommended.

The trailhead is on the grounds of private Ferndale Ranch, adjacent to Thomas Aquinas College. Follow Highway 126 from Ventura to the town of Santa Paula and take the 10th Street/Highway 150 exit toward Ojai. Travel northwest on Highway 150 about 6 miles to the signed entrance gates at Ferndale Ranch and Thomas Aquinas College. Turn right at the first one and follow the paved drive through the college campus for a half-mile to a paved spur on the right, which leads uphill a short distance to a locked gate. Park in the turnout near the gate, being careful not to block any of the driveways. The trail begins on the other side of the gate. No water or restrooms are available.

Description

Beyond the gate, bear left on the paved road as it leads downhill through the ranch. Go right when the road forks at 0.2 mile, passing a complex of oil storage tanks and pumps, and bear right at the next road junction, heading uphill past oak trees, sycamores and cottonwoods. At 0.6 mile the road ends at a fence surrounding another complex of oil pumps on a bench above the creek. The trail goes to the left, skirting the fenced enclosure. The cliff face near the wells displays folded layers of sedimentary rocks, which have been bowed up here by the pressure of movement along nearby fault lines.

At 0.6 miles a driveway takes off to the left and crosses the creek before entering private ranch land. Continue to the right, following the course of the creek through thick riparian growth overhanging its pools and cascades.

At 1.1 miles, the trail crosses the stream and passes through a jumble of small boulders before climbing away from the water to meet another dirt road at 1.2 miles. Go right on the road. The canyon soon opens up, and on the slopes to your right can be seen small groves of big-cone Douglas fir, also known as big-cone spruce. The drier south-facing slope on the left supports a few oaks and some desert-dwelling yucca and prickly-pear cactus.

Stay on the road, ignoring the faint trail on the left at 1.6 miles, and return to the creek's bank at 1.9 miles. The canyon begins to narrow again, and the vegetation begins to crowd in. Cross the stream again at 2.1 miles, enjoying the shade of leafy alders and cottonwoods, and begin a moderate ascent of the slope above the creek. Good views open up almost immediately, allowing an examination of the layered rock walls of the canyon.

The climb tops out at 2.9 miles, and the trail descends gently to the forested flat occupied by Big Cone Camp, at 3 miles. The scent of evergreens fills the air at this pleasant campground, which has five sites.

Continue through the camp and descend steeply on a loose, rocky trail to the bank of East Fork Santa Paula Creek. Follow the trail downstream about 50 yards and cross, scrambling over the rocks and turning north to follow the main canyon. The trail climbs and then descends to a sandy beach at the edge of a

deep pool at 3.1 miles. A lovely waterfall drops about 20 feet into the pool, which invites you to take a cooling dip.

After a refreshing pause to enjoy the music of canyon wrens and falling water, return the way you came. ■

**Waterfall on
East Fork
Santa Paula Creek**

Hike #31: Twin Forks

Distance	5.6 miles
Level of difficulty	Moderate
Child rating	10 and up
Starting elevation	3000 feet
Highest point on trail	3550 feet
Topographic map	Lion Canyon 7.5′
Guidebook map	17

Chumash rock art, spectacular cliffs of gleaming white sandstone and a pleasant year-round stream are highlights of the trail to Twin Forks backcountry camp, one of the most enjoyable hikes in Los Padres National Forest.

The trailhead is on the banks of famed Sespe Creek, a Wild and Scenic River popular with catch-and-release fly fishers for its small but lively population of wild trout. To reach it, take Highway 33 north from Ventura and follow it 28 miles as it climbs high into the rugged mountains north of Ojai. Turn right onto Rose Valley Road and follow this narrow, paved track 6 miles to its end at Lion Camp on the edge of Sespe Creek. Park in the day-use parking area at the east end of the campground, which has pit toilets but no water.

Although the campground is open year-round, the road is sometimes barred in winter by a locked gate 1 mile from the trailhead.

Description

The trail leads north from the campground next to a sign and restroom, dropping into the creek bed and crossing the stream. During winter and spring, when the creek is engorged with runoff, this can be a wet crossing. In summer, it's a matter of hopping a few rocks.

On the other side of the creek, the trail splits next to a sign. Go left, beginning a moderate climb across a chaparral-covered slope toward the striking outcrops of pale sandstone visible just ahead. The feature is known as Piedra Blanca ("white rock" in Spanish) and has given its name to a trail camp and to the creek you'll soon be following.

The rocky trail, broad and well-maintained, descends into a gully and climbs out the other side at 0.5 mile, reaching a junction about 50 yards beyond. Go right, crossing the boundary of the new Sespe Wilderness area, established in 1992, and reaching the edge of the Piedra Blanca rock formations at 0.8 mile. For the next 0.4 mile the trail winds among these huge, weirdly eroded cliffs and boulders, offering innumerable opportunities for exploration and play. The slopes are rounded and easy to climb, and in many places cavities have been eroded into the rock, making perfect hiding places for young trekkers.

At 1.3 miles the trail drops sharply into a ravine north of the boulder field, crossing a trickle of water and then heading northwest up the course of Piedra Blanca Creek over cobbles and sand. At 1.5 miles you cross a ledge above the creek and then descend to its banks under the shade of large oak and sycamore trees.

The trail climbs again at 2 miles, working its way along the canyon wall above the creek. At 2.7 miles it climbs over a ridge and begins a sharp descent to the creek and Twin Forks trail camp, at 2.8 miles.

The camp has several sites with fire pits, and is shaded by huge oak trees. Toward the south end of the camp, which is strung out along the bank of Piedra Blanca Creek, is a prominent boulder with a pair of depressions on its face. In each are several painted figures, some of them abstract but at least one resembling a salamander or a similar creature. Nearby is a metal box containing a trail register and information about these Chumash pictographs.

Visitors are welcome to examine the paintings, which may be hundreds of years old, but should not touch them. Even the innocent dab of a fingertip against the fragile paint leaves a deposit of oil and sweat that hastens deterioration. These rare and mysterious artworks, left here by a vanished people, are an irreplaceable part of the nation's cultural heritage and deserve respect and protection.

The camp makes a good place to stop for a picnic lunch and a dip in the clear, cool water of Piedra Blanca Creek. Energetic hikers may continue up the trail another 2.5 miles to Pine Mountain Camp, 2500 feet higher up the forested slopes. If that doesn't appeal to you, turn around and retrace your steps to the trailhead. ■

Hike #32: Wheeler Gorge Nature Trail

Distance	1 mile
Level of difficulty	Easy
Child rating	3 and up
Starting elevation	1800 feet
Highest point on trail	2000 feet
Topographic map	Wheeler Springs 7.5′
Guidebook map	19

This short, easy trail keyed to an interpretive brochure offers an excellent introduction to the plants of the chaparral and riparian zones in Los Padres National Forest. It is especially attractive if you are camping at the popular Wheeler Gorge Campground, which is within walking distance of the trailhead.

To reach the trail, take Highway 33 north from the Highway 101 freeway in Ventura and follow it 22 miles to the Wheeler Gorge Campground. As you pass the campground entrance, begin looking on your left for a turnout next to a locked gate, about half a mile north. Park in the turnout, being sure not to block the gate. A large sign marks the trailhead and has a dispenser for the interpretive brochures.

The campground has restrooms and water.

Description

The trail dips toward the creek and crosses underneath the highway bridge, threading its way through a healthy stand of poison oak as it follows the course of North Fork Matilija Creek, crossing at 0.1 mile. The stream is well shaded by cottonwoods, sycamores and oaks.

There are many informal side trails cut over the years by anglers and kids playing in the stream, but the main trail is easy to follow by keeping watch for the numbered signs keyed to the leaflet.

At 0.3 mile, the trail turns and follows a tiny tributary creek, passing sycamores and toyon. It climbs to a low ridge at 0.5 and reaches a junction with one of the many faint tracks around the creek; bear left, beginning to circle back toward the road and descending across a rocky hillside covered with chamise and laurel sumac.

The trail returns to the creek at 0.9 mile and crosses, reaching the trailhead at 1 mile. ■

How perfectly enchanting and care-obliterating
are these withdrawn gardens of the woods —
long vistas opening to the sea —
sunshine sifting and pouring upon the flowery ground
in a tremulous, shifting mosaic,
as the light-ways in the leafy wall open and close
with the swaying breeze —
shining leaves and flowers, birds and bees,
mingling together in springtime harmony,
and soothing fragrance exhaling
from a thousand thousand fountains!
In these balmy dissolving days,
when the deep heart-beats of Nature are felt
thrilling the rocks and trees and everything alike,
common business and friends are happily forgotten,
and even the natural honey-work of bees,
and the care of birds for their young,
and mothers for their children,
seem slightly out of place.

——John Muir,
writing of springtime in the forests of the Coast Ranges,
from *The Mountains of California*

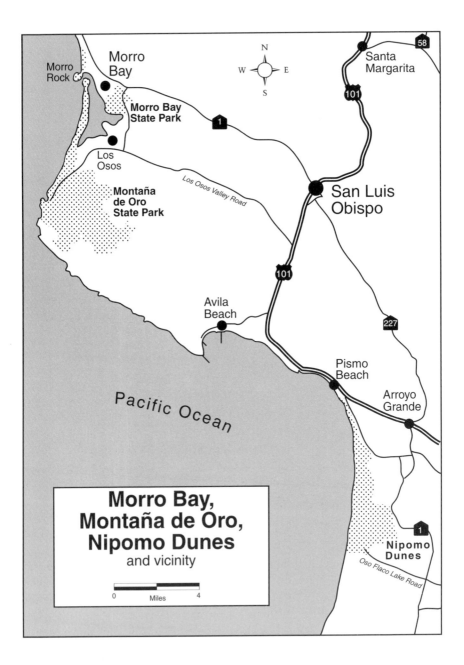

Morro Rock
Morro Bay
Morro Bay State Park
Los Osos
Montaña de Oro State Park
Los Osos Valley Road
Santa Margarita
San Luis Obispo
Avila Beach
Pacific Ocean
Pismo Beach
Arroyo Grande
Nipomo Dunes
Oso Flaco Lake Road

N
W E
S

58
101
1
227
1

Morro Bay, Montaña de Oro, Nipomo Dunes
and vicinity

0   Miles   4

Morro Bay and Montaña de Oro State Parks

Geological History

Sharing a common boundary and administered in tandem by the California Department of Parks and Recreation, Morro Bay and Montaña de Oro are like siblings, their relationship cemented by the common influence of the sea.

With 7 miles of shoreline, 8,000-acre Montaña de Oro State Park contains sandy little pocket beaches where pounding waves have carved small coves into the rocky bluffs. Farther inland, ancient sand dunes long forsaken by the surf hide beneath coverings of hardy scrub. The air is always filled with the white-noise wash of waves against land, and the cries of gulls are a constant accompaniment.

But even in its inland reaches, where small creeks trickle through steep-walled canyons and mountain peaks rise abruptly to more than 1,600 feet, the sea makes its presence felt, and not only in the way it flavors the air with salt tang and sends tendrils of fog slipping over the summits. The very rocks of the hills and canyons are its legacy: pale layers of shale, thousands of feet thick, recording a time when the region lay at the bottom of the ocean.

Almost the entire park is built of this formation, known as Monterey shale. It consists of solidified mud, silt and sand, mixed with the remains of tiny marine organisms such as diatoms and plankton. It dates to the Miocene epoch, around 20 million years ago, and it records millions of years of deposition.

The once-horizontal beds were contorted, shoved upward to form the park's mountainous interior. They are folded and tilted, in some places standing nearly vertical. The deformation of this old sea bottom is the result of a collision between great plates of Earth's crust, in restless motion as they float on molten rock below. Erosion by streams and by storm runoff has carved deep valleys into the mountains' flanks, exposing hundreds of feet of thinly bedded sedimentary rock interlaced with the fossils of mollusks and other organisms.

South of the visitor center, the park's crumpled topography gives way near the shore to a broad, flat tableland, a marine terrace with sheer bluffs overlooking the surf. This broad plain marks the old shore, having been worn smooth by waves when the landscape lay at sea level. Subsequent uplift caused by the continuing pressure of tectonic collision raised it beyond the reach of the surf. Careful examination reveals other marine terraces well up on the slopes of Valencia Peak.

Reminders of an earlier time are also preserved north of park headquarters. Ancient sand dunes, now high above sea level and well inland from the water, lie almost hidden there beneath a thick mantle of shrubs, trees and grasses. Although old for dunes — perhaps 5,000 years — they are geologically quite young when compared to the sea sediments found atop the nearby peaks.

Morro Bay State Park, hemmed in on one side by a bay and on the other by a large coastal marsh, shares most of Montaña de Oro's geological history, with one important exception: the string of *morros*, a Spanish term for rounded hills, that reach inland from prominent Morro Rock at the entrance to Morro Bay. Each is a plug of 25 million-year-old dacite, a volcanic rock, and represents the throat of a long-vanished volcano. The ancient magma solidified not far below the surface and has been exposed through erosion of the overlying layers of shale and other rocks.

There are nine major *morros* lined up in a gently curving arc between Morro Bay and San Luis Obispo, and several smaller intrusions of the same material poking up through the coastal hills. In Morro Bay State Park they are represented by Morro Rock, Black Hill and Cerro Cabrillo; moving on to the southeast the string includes Cerro Romualdo, Chumash Peak, Bishop Peak and Cerro San Luis Obispo.

The likeliest explanation for these formations is that a line of volcanoes once dominated the skyline of coastal San Luis Obispo County, spewing ash, cinders and lava flows over the countryside. Sedimentary layers in the area preserve some of this material, but most has been removed by erosion, leaving little but the resistant plugs as evidence.

Human History

Human beings have called this part of the Central Coast home for more than 8,000 years. The first inhabitants enjoyed a wetter environment and relied extensively on seeds and other plant food. Then the climate grew drier and warmer, and the inhabitants grew to rely more on shellfish and fish. By about 1,000 years ago, the region was home to people known as the Chumash, whose territory extended from Malibu in the south to Morro Bay on the north.

Like all coastal Chumash bands, the inhabitants of the Morro Bay-Montaña de Oro area relied heavily on the sea for subsistence, consuming a wide variety of marine species. They supplemented their diet with seeds and acorns gathered from inland grasslands and oak groves, as well as with terrestrial and marine mammals, and they were part of a vast trade network that extended well into the desert Southwest. Although there has been little archaeological research in the parks themselves, evidence of village sites and thick deposits of household trash, called middens, can be found in many places: Shell fragments litter the ground around the old ranch house that serves as park headquarters in Montaña de Oro, an extensive midden lies in the old dunes north of Islay Creek, and remnants of a village are on the bluff overlooking the mouth of Coon Creek. Middens and grinding holes worn into boulders are also visible on the slopes of Turtle Rock in Morro Bay.

Spanish explorers visited the area for the first time in 1542, when Juan Rodriguez Cabrillo led a seafaring expedition along the California coast from Mexico to the Oregon border. During his voyage, Cabrillo named Morro Rock, which served as a landmark for other expeditions that passed by during the next two centuries.

Europeans did not arrive by land in significant numbers until 1769. That year the Gaspar de Portolá expedition, dispatched from San Diego to blaze an overland route to the Spanish settlement at Monterey Bay, struggled through difficult and swampy terrain on their way from what is now San Luis Obispo to Morro Bay. The name of the nearby community of Los Osos ("The bears") commemorates the killing of a grizzly bear in the vicinity by members of the expedition.

Following in the footsteps of Portolá were members of the Franciscan order, who established a mission at San Luis Obispo in 1772. The missionaries, aided by Spanish soldiers, rounded up most of the surrounding Chumash and brought them into the settlement that grew up around the mission. There they were converted to Christianity and put to work raising food and performing other tasks for the economic support of the mission and the salvation of their souls.

Few survived the experience. Disease and malnutrition devastated the Chumash, as they did the native people throughout California. The population plummeted, and by the time the mission lands were taken away from the church by the civilian government and distributed among private ranch owners, the Chumash culture was all but extinct.

The Montaña de Oro and Morro Bay lands were divided in the early 1840s among several great ranchos, which were used to graze cattle for the lucrative hide-and-tallow trade. Following California statehood in 1850, the ranchos were broken up and sold off, frequently to pay legal bills related to settlement of contested land claims.

In 1892, Alden B. Spooner, Jr., leased 6,500 acres of the Pecho y Islay Rancho around Islay Creek in Montaña de Oro, and built barns and a ranch house. He later added a creamery, stables and a waterwheel for power. He raised dairy cattle and hogs, and built a warehouse and loading chute on the bluff so produce could be loaded onto schooners moored in the cove that now bears his name. The Spooner ranch house now serves as park headquarters and visitor center.

Ranch land north of Islay Creek was owned by Alexander Hazard, who also raised crops and ran a dairy. Hoping to cash in on the region's growing demand for timber, he planted rows of fast-growing eucalyptus trees in Hazard Canyon. The trees turned out to be useless for lumber, but remain standing today, where they host great flocks of migrating monarch butterflies between October and March.

Spooner eventually purchased the land he'd been leasing and later added to his holdings by acquiring neighboring property. His heirs sold out to rancher Oscar C. Fields in the 1940s; Fields in turn sold the land to Irene McAllister, who gave it the name it still bears: Montaña de Oro, Mountain of Gold, for the vast sprays of poppies and other wildflowers that carpet the hillsides in springtime.

McAllister's ranch went into bankruptcy in the 1960s, and in 1965 the state acquired it for preservation as a park.

Morro Bay became an important seaport during the late 1800s; the harbor was never very easy to enter, but the nearest railway line was hundreds of miles away and local settlers had little choice. The town was founded in 1870 by homesteader Franklin Riley, and the town quickly grew up around its crucial wharf, which handled shipments of wool, potatoes, barley and dairy products from surrounding farms.

The state acquired land for the park in the 1930s, and the Civilian Conservation Corps planted the groves of eucalyptus that still shade the campground. The CCC crews also improved the public golf course and campground facilities, and built the causeway linking Morro Rock to the mainland. In recent years, additional acreage has been added to the southeast part of the park, incorporating former ranchland around Cerro Cabrillo.

Morro Rock itself, having been quarried for many years to provide the raw materials of jetties and breakwaters throughout the region, was declared a state historical landmark in 1968 and is now the center of Morro Rock Ecological Preserve, set aside to protect nesting peregrine falcons and seabirds.

Plants and Animals

Montaña de Oro and Morro Bay encompass a surprising diversity of ecosystems, from riparian communities along the small creeks, to coastal chaparral on the mountain slopes, acres of rocky tidepools along the shoreline and the largest undisturbed coastal marsh complex in California.

The waters are home to some of the most engaging creatures of the Pacific. The southern sea otter, once rendered nearly extinct by hunters seeking its luxurious pelt, has made a modest comeback along the Central Coast and may be spotted foraging for shellfish in the waters between the surf and the kelp line at Montaña de Oro. Voracious feeders, they consume as much as a quarter of their body weight (which ranges from 40 pounds for adult females to more than 60 pounds for males) each day in the form of abalone, crabs, clams, lobsters and other delicacies.

In fall and spring, Pacific gray whales may be seen just offshore, particularly from the bluffs of Montaña de Oro. The great marine mammals migrate each year between food-rich Alaskan waters and the protected lagoons of Baja California, where they give birth. Visitors may also spot harbor seals, which favor a reef near Corallina Cove as a spot to sun themselves.

On land, the parks host raccoons, coyotes, foxes, rabbits, deer, an occasional bobcat and mountain lion, and many varieties of rodents. They are also great places for bird-watching, as turkey vultures skim the ridgelines, and raptors, from the northern harrier to red-tailed hawks, patrol the mountain slopes in search of prey. Along the shore, seabirds such as cormorants and several species of gulls — western, California and herring — call the parks home.

Morro Bay offers bird watchers two other special treats: A pair of rare peregrine falcons nest seasonally on Morro Rock, and the eucalyptus groves just north of the park's museum hosts a huge rookery for great blue herons, which nest and rear their young between January and August.

The parks are no less diverse in their plant offerings. Along the creeks grows a wild profusion of plants, including willow trees, cottonwoods, wild cucumber vines, hedge nettle and the ubiquitous poison oak, which attains great lushness and menaces hikers by reaching into the trails. The oil in its leaves and stems is a powerful irritant and can produce a painful, itching rash. In the shade, the tree limbs are often bedecked with ghostly strands of lace lichen, which is actually a fungus living in symbiotic harmony with a variety of algae: the fungus provides a moist foundation for the algae, which in turn produce food for their host.

Along the wind-swept mountain slopes, dry and exposed to the sun, a chaparral community of tough, drought-resistant shrubs and grasses has evolved. Woody perennials such as chamise, ceanothus, buckwheat, manzanita, sage, tree poppy and bush monkeyflower form a thick tangle taller than a person. On the open, rocky hillsides, particularly near the peaks, the ground is carpeted by grasses and wildflowers that put on a spectacular show in springtime: poppies, lupine, blue dicks, paintbrush, black mustard. In secluded pockets of the mountains are groves of old oak trees and stands of Bishop pine.

Access

Montaña de Oro lies on the coast just west of the university town of San Luis Obispo. To reach it, take the Los Osos Valley Road exit off Highway 101 in San Luis Obispo, and follow it 10 miles to the town of Los Osos. Turn left on Pecho Valley Road and follow it into the park.

Morro Bay State Park is just north of Montaña de Oro. Northbound travelers on the Highway 101 freeway should take the Highway 1 exit in San Luis Obispo and drive 13 miles northwest to South Bay Boulevard, turn right and drive another half-mile to the park entrance. If you are traveling south on Highway 101, take the Highway 41 exit in Atascadero and follow it 16 miles southwest to Highway 1. Take Highway 1 south about 1 mile to South Bay Boulevard.

Visitor Centers

Montaña de Oro has a single visitor center, also the location of park headquarters. It occupies the old Spooner ranch house and is at the entrance to the park campground, across the road from Spooner Cove. It offers a modest selection of literature about park features, and a small display of material relating to the park's geology, prehistory and history. Its hours vary with the season: 11 A.M. to 3 P.M. Friday through Sunday in the winter, spring and fall; and noon to 4 P.M. daily between Memorial Day and Labor Day. Ranger-led campfire talks about the park's natural history are offered during the summer, and docents lead talks and hikes year round. Check the bulletin board near the visitor center for dates and times.

At Morro Bay, the Museum of Natural History offers informative displays and a wide selection of publications about the wildlife, history and ecology of the Central Coast. Situated on a scenic bluff overlooking the bay, it also hosts slide shows, lectures, puppet shows, movies and field outings.

The museum is open from 10 A.M. to 5 P.M. daily, except on Thanksgiving, Christmas and New Year's Day. Admission is $2.

Campgrounds

In Montaña de Oro, there is a single campground for visitors with vehicles, containing 50 sites, in the canyon behind the Spooner ranch house. Vault toilets, water and trash bins are provided. Each site has a picnic table and fire pit. There are no showers or dump stations, and the length limit for trailers and motorhomes is 24 feet. The fee is $7 a night. There is no park entrance fee. Spaces are available on a first-come, first-served basis except during the summer (Memorial Day to Labor Day), when they may be reserved through the DESTINET system.

There are also four primitive "environmental" walk-in campsites located along Pecho Valley Road, each of which can accommodate a single small group. Each has a tent site, pit toilet and picnic table but no water. Reservations are required, and may be made through the DESTINET system. The fee is $11 on weekends and $10 during the week.

For horseback riders, there are five sites in a reservation-only horse camp a quarter mile south of the park entrance on Pecho Valley Road. The camp has pipe corrals, plenty of room for horse trailers, tables, pit toilets and water. The fee varies with the size of the site and the number of horses, starting at $18 a night for the smaller sites and $50 for the larger ones. DESTINET handles reservations for these sites as well.

At Morro Bay, the camping experience is somewhat more luxurious. There are 135 sites nestled in a pine and eucalyptus forest. Each site has a food locker, table and fire pit; 20 sites have full water and electrical hookups. Buildings with restrooms, hot showers and laundry tubs are provided, as is a dump station for trailers and recreational vehicles. There are two group camps with a capacity of 30 and 50 people each.

The fee for individual sites is $17 a night on weekdays and $18 on weekends, and reservations are recommended. They may be made through the DESTINET system.

Food, Gas and Lodging.

Montaña de Oro offers no services. Stores, gas stations and motels are available in the nearby communities of Los Osos, Morro Bay and San Luis Obispo. In Morro Bay State Park, a café next to the small-boat marina offers meals and beverages. There is also a pro shop and clubhouse at the park's 18-hole public golf course.

Phone Numbers and Addresses

Montaña de Oro: For recorded information, call (805) 528-0513. To reserve sites in the horse camps and environmental camps year-round, and sites in the main campground during the summer, call DESTINET, the state park reservation system, at (800) 444-7275 between 8 A.M. and 5 P.M. weekdays. For general park information, call (805) 772-7434 between 9 A.M. and 3 P.M. daily or write to park headquarters at Montaña de Oro, Pecho Valley Road, Los Osos, CA 93442.

Morro Bay: For recorded information, call (805) 772-2560. For campground reservations, call DESTINET at (800) 444-7275. For general park information, call (805) 772-7434 or (805) 549-3312, or write to park headquarters at Morro Bay State Park, State Park Road, Morro Bay, CA 93442. To contact the museum, call (805) 772-2694. ∎

Trails of Morro Bay

 Hiking is not the primary attraction at Morro Bay State Park, where birding, beachcombing, boating, kayaking and even golf vie for visitors' attention. It has several short trails, however, which offer a chance to explore its interesting geology and which provide delightful views of its harbor, the rolling countryside nearby, the expansive marsh and estuary that distinguish it from all other coastal parks, and the signature rock looming over the entrance to the bay.

Birders will especially enjoy the wide variety of species that visit or make their home at Morro Bay — some 200 in all, including herons and egrets, which have established a rookery in the eucalyptus grove on the bay's east shore. The park is also an ideal place for families, with its gentle terrain, ranges of amenities and proximity to nearby towns. Visitors intending to camp or to stay overnight in nearby motels should bear in mind the park's popularity and make sure to secure reservations.

None of these hikes requires special preparation, but coastal weather is always variable — sunny mornings can give way to foggy afternoons, and vice-versa — so it is always advisable to carry a jacket or sweater. ■

Hike #33: Black Hill

Distance	2.4 miles
Level of difficulty	Moderate
Child rating	5 and up
Starting elevation	120 feet
Highest point on trail	661 feet
Topographic map	Morro Bay South 7.5′
Guidebook map	20

Morro Bay gets its name from Morro Rock, the large, volcanic plug at its entrance. Black Hill is the second such volcanic peak in a line reaching from west to east. This moderately steep hike to its summit offers grand views of the Morro Bay region and a closer look at the feldspar-rich volcanic rock that comprises these prominent landmarks.

The trailhead is on View Drive east of the park's golf course. To reach it, enter the park from South Bay Boulevard and bear right at the first intersection. Park in the wide turnout used for overflow parking on the south side of the road and walk about a 0.1 mile to where the trail intersects the pavement. A sign here says the trail is closed to bicycle traffic. Water and restrooms are available in the campground.

Description

The sandy trail climbs moderately through sage scrub, a plant community that includes coyote brush, black sage, bush monkeyflower and various grasses. There's a grove of fragrant eucalyptus trees to the left; to the right is a good view of the marshes and meandering channels of the Morro Bay estuary.

At 0.3 mile, oak trees and ferns join the plant community. The trail levels out and then drops into a ravine, where it meets another trail coming in from the right. Go left, climb into a grove of eucalyptus and pass the site of an old pump house on the left.

Beyond the pump house the trail reaches another junction. Bear right, climbing more steeply as you work your way up toward a grove of pine trees. There are several faint use trails crossing the main path, but the route is clear, leading toward a large concrete water tank at 0.9 mile. There's an outcropping of dacite near the tank, beyond which the trail switchbacks until reaching a parking area just below the summit.

Past the parking area, the trail climbs swiftly to the summit, at 1.2 miles. The views are well worth the climb, extending 360 degrees and taking in

Morro Bay, the coastline as far north as Point Sal, the mountains of
Montaña de Oro on the south, and inland past the coastal valleys to the
distant Santa Lucia Range.

Return the way you came.   ■

Morro Rock, seen from the top of Black Hill

Hike #34: Quarry Trail

Distance	2 miles
Level of difficulty	Easy
Child rating	5 and up
Starting elevation	20 feet
Highest point on trail	329 feet
Topographic map	Morro Bay South 7.5'
Guidebook map	20

The Quarry Trail traverses a relatively recent addition to Morro Bay State Park, former ranchland added in two phases in the 1970s and 1980s. The terrain is rolling grassland, punctuated by rounded hills of volcanic origin, along the edge of the Morro Bay estuary. This loop samples the diversity of plant life in the park and offers good views of the coastal marsh.

The trailhead is at a parking area on the east side of Bay Boulevard a half-mile south of the entrance to Morro Bay State Park. There is ample parking, but no water or restrooms. The trail begins next to a sign that provides maps, historical information and a photographic guide to the wildflowers of the area.

Description

The trail leads east from the parking area, climbing gently through sage scrub at the foot of Cerro Cabrillo, a 911-foot high plug of volcanic rock. At 0.25 mile the trail reaches the beginning of the quarry, where blocks of the 25-million-year-old dacite were blasted out of the hillside in 1959 to be used in construction of a new stretch of Highway 1 between Pennington Creek and Morro Bay. Cliff swallows have built nests in the face of the fractured rock, and provide an entertaining aerial display in the spring.

At 0.5 mile the trail reaches a junction. Go right, following the Live Oak Trail south as it crosses a wide, grassy hillside and reaches a junction at 0.6 mile with a spur leading to the top of Portola Point, the rounded hill to the right. Turn here and follow the spur as it switchbacks up the slope through thick stands of black sage, poison oak, bush monkeyflower and paintbrush.

At 0.9 mile the trail splits. Go right, circling the crown of the hill and reaching the summit at 1 mile. The view is quite nice, encompassing Morro Bay and the extensive coastal wetlands on its east end. This complex system of marshland and creeks, where salt and fresh water mingle under the fluctuating influence of the tides, is among the largest undisturbed estuarine ecosystems on the Pacific coast.

Complete the loop around the summit and follow the trail back down to the Live Oak Trail, which you reach at 1.3 miles. Go right, descending sharply into a ravine where pools of water sometimes collect.

At 1.5 miles you reach a junction. Turn right, climb about 50 yards and then begin contouring along a grassy hillside. At 1.7 miles the trail drops to a bench above the highway and follows a level course. At 1.8 miles it leaves the bench and drops back to the south side of the parking area, reaching the starting point at 2 miles.   ■

Hike #35: Turtle Rock

Distance	1.2 miles
Level of difficulty	Easy
Child rating	5 and up
Starting elevation	80 feet
Highest point on trail	209 feet
Topographic map	Morro Bay South 7.5′
Guidebook map	20

This short hike involves a scramble over boulders to reach the top of a rounded knob between Black Hill and Cerro Cabrillo, two of the volcanic plugs arrayed between Morro Rock and San Luis Obispo. The view from the top of Turtle Rock is hardly worth the climb, but the trail leads past a Chumash midden and several bedrock mortars, evidence of prehistoric human habitation that will interest students of native cultures.

To reach the trailhead, drive to the Morro Bay State Park entrance and park on the shoulder of the park road. Walk back out to South Bay Boulevard and head south across the bridge over Chorro Creek. On the east side of the road is a driveway barred by a locked gate with NO PARKING signs on it.

Description

Follow the driveway past the locked gate. The road leads moderately uphill along the course of Chorro Creek, through lush vegetation. At 0.2 mile the road forks; stay to the right, continuing up the hillside past wild cucumber, poison oak and dusty miller, nearing a fence and a locked gate at 0.4 mile. The property beyond is privately owned and public entry is prohibited.

Just before the fence, the trail branches off the road to the left, squeezing through dense brush as it begins ascending the hill. The ground here is littered with fragments of clam and abalone shells discarded by the Chumash. Judging by the quantity of debris, thick deposits of which are visible on the private property beyond the gate, this was the site of a permanent encampment of considerable size.

About 50 yards from the road, the trail forks. Stay to the left and climb up the rocky hillside. Additional evidence of permanent Chumash settlement appears a few yards farther along, where large, pinkish boulders of feldspar-rich dacite — magma that hardened within the throat of a vanished volcano — crop out of the hill beneath the shade of a large pine tree. Careful scouting reveals several deep mortars worn into the large boulders next to the trail. Chumash women spent long hours here, grinding acorns, grass seeds and pine nuts into flour with stone pestles.

The trail fades as it enters the boulder field and some scrambling is required to reach the summit at 0.6 mile. The attraction of this spot is plain: Tall pines shade the hilltop, which catches the sea breeze and offers a nice view of the Morro Bay estuary. It does not take much imagination to envision groups of women from the nearby Chumash settlement gathering here to seek shelter from the warm summer sun, swapping stories while performing their essential domestic tasks.

Return the way you came.   ■

Coastal marsh along Morro Bay, seen from Turtle Rock

Trails of Montaña de Oro State Park

The trails of Montaña de Oro offer a range of experiences, guaranteeing something for just about everyone. Those who want expansive views will find routes leading to the tops of rocky peaks; wildflower fans will find what they seek in the hilly inland meadows; those in search of bird and marine life will find it along the bluffs that look out over the surf and the rocky coves.

A few words of warning are in order. Dogs are not allowed on any of the trails in the park. Ticks may be found in the tall grass along the trails. Rattlesnakes, while seldom seen, are part of the local fauna. And poison oak is probably the most common form of plant life in the park, taking a variety of forms from crawling vine to thick shrub. Its leaves range in color from shiny green to bright red, but all contain an unpleasant chemical that causes a nasty rash in those who are susceptible. Before starting out on any of the park trails, learn to identify it. The visitor center has informative displays.

After a hike, especially through the lower and wetter areas, it's sensible to wash exposed skin with strong soap to remove any lingering traces of the plant's irritating oil. It's probably also a good idea to do a quick check for ticks, which will cling to the skin for as long as several hours before actually biting. Check especially around constricted points, such as cuffs and waistband, which often block the insects as they crawl upward seeking a dark and warm place to latch on.

The trails described in the following pages sample all the major types of terrain and life zone preserved in Montaña de Oro: coastal bluffs, mountain peaks, creekside corridors, meadows and sand dunes. Summer days can be quite warm; spring and autumn days often grow suddenly cold and windy in the afternoons. Always carry water. If you are embarking on a hike of more than an hour or two, it's a good idea to pack a sweater or jacket. ■

Hike #36: Bluffs Trail

Distance	3.4 miles
Level of difficulty	Easy
Child rating	5 and up
Starting elevation	50 feet
Highest point on trail	50 feet
Topographic map	Morro Bay South 7.5′
Guidebook map	21

This easy route along a broad terrace overlooking the sea offers a chance to enjoy Montaña de Oro's lovely scenery and remarkable array of wildlife without much exertion, and provides a perfect outing for those with young children, limited time, or both.

The trailhead is a dirt pullout on the west side of Pecho Valley Road about 100 yards south of the entrance to the campground and visitor center. Park there or in the visitor center lot.

Grotto Rock, as seen from the Bluffs Trail

Description

Follow the well-defined trail as it crosses a wooden bridge and leads toward the ocean. Stay left at the first fork just beyond the bridge. The trail is broad and easy to follow, receiving a great deal of use from hikers and bicyclists. It crosses a broad meadow carpeted with hardy grasses, wild radish and New Zealand spinach, passes a pair of outhouses at 0.3 mile and reaches a junction with a trail that crosses a bridge to the right and heads back to Spooner Cove. Stay to the left, reaching the edge of the bluffs above Corallina Cove at 0.6 mile. The cove contains rocky reefs with many tidepools, and often boasts a population of harbor seals. Watch also for the occasional sea otter floating on its back between the surf and the kelp line, balancing a rock on its chest and using it to crack the shells of its favorite foods: crabs, mussels, abalone, lobsters.

The trail turns south here and parallels the edge of the bluffs, crossing paths every quarter-mile that lead back to the park road. At 1.7 miles the trail reaches a steel fence marking the park boundary. Grotto Rock, a castle-shaped prominence with sea caves eroded into its face, is to the right; beyond the fence lies the mouth of Coon Creek, Point Buchon and the property of Pacific Gas & Electric Co., which operates the Diablo Canyon nuclear power plant less than 4 miles to the south. The plant's presence is responsible for the warning signs located at various places throughout the park telling visitors what to do if they hear a loud and steady siren blast for 3 to 5 minutes (tune radios to 920 or 1400 AM, or 98.1 FM, for information).

Turn around here at the fence and return the way you came. ■

Valencia Peak rising above the rocky shoreline of Montaña de Oro State Park

Hike #37: Dunes Trail

Distance	3.4 miles
Level of difficulty	Easy
Child rating	5 and up
Starting elevation	80 feet
Highest point on trail	120 feet
Topographic map	Morro Bay South 7.5'
Guidebook map	21

This relatively easy stroll through scrub-covered sand dunes extending north of Spooner Cove on a bluff above the shoreline offers visitors a chance to explore a rare, undamaged relic of another time. The dunes were built over many thousands of years by stiff onshore winds. They have been raised well above sea level now and are no longer growing or moving. A dense stabilizing growth of coastal dune scrub, including ceanothus, sagebrush, lupine, buckwheat and coyote brush covers the sand, which is home to a variety of insects and rodents. The tracks of these creatures may be seen in the trail early in the day, before the feet of hikers and horses have erased them. Also hidden in the dune sand are ancient trash piles called middens, where the Chumash camped and left great piles of shell fragments.

Description

The trailhead is on the west side of Pecho Valley Road on the bluff just north of Spooner Cove, about 100 yards from the entrance to the visitor center and campground. There is a fork immediately beyond the sign that marks the start of the trail; bear right on the gravelly tread, climbing slightly and crossing an open meadow with a pleasing view of the ocean. At 0.1 mile the trail enters the soft dune sand, and walking becomes fairly laborious even though the path is level.

Faint tracks crisscross the main trail throughout the dunes, cut by casual foot traffic. Ignore them and stay on the main path, which parallels the shoreline between the cliff and the park road. At 0.5 mile a trail crosses the main trail, leading from the park road to the beach. Continue straight ahead, obeying the warning signs that caution against leaving the trail and trampling the fragile vegetation.

At 1 mile, the trail is joined by a spur from the right that leads back to a parking area for horseback riders at the side of the road. Past this junction the trail descends sharply on a series of steps to a small creek that cuts through the bluffs and empties in the ocean at Hazard Canyon Reef. The trail crosses the creek on a small boardwalk and climbs the other side of the canyon. At the top of the bluff, a short spur to the left leads to an overlook with a good view of the coastline north and south.

The main trail skirts the edge of a eucalyptus grove, the remains of a failed effort at timber production in the 19th century. The grove now serves another purpose, hosting great swarms of monarch butterflies during the winter stopover on their annual migration.

At 1.2 miles the trail forks; bear right, staying near the eucalyptus grove and climbing steadily. The trail reaches its highest point at 1.3 miles, offering a terrific view of Morro Rock, an ancient plug of lava, and Morro Bay, as well as the long sandspit that separates the bay and its expansive estuary from the sea. The trail then descends, reaching another junction at 1.7 miles, within sight of the intersection of Pecho Valley Road and Sandspit road about 100 yards to the northeast. Turn left here, heading toward the ocean.

At 2 miles the trail comes to a three-way junction. Continue straight ahead about 50 yards for a nice view of the shoreline, and then backtrack to the junction, turning right this time and heading south, back in the direction of park headquarters. This small loop ends at 2.2 miles when your path rejoins the main trail. From here, retrace the route you followed on the outbound leg of the hike, returning to your starting point at 3.4 miles. ∎

Hike #38: Hazard Peak

Distance	8 miles
Level of difficulty	Strenuous
Child rating	10 and up
Starting elevation	80 feet
Highest point on trail	1076 feet
Topographic map	Morro Bay South 7.5'
Guidebook map	21

This loop through the heart of Montaña de Oro is among the best the park has to offer. It begins by following a lush riparian corridor, climbs onto windswept hills and returns along a ridgetop route with spectacular views of the coastline and the inland mountains.

The trailhead is at a pullout just north of Islay Creek, on a bluff overlooking the entrance to the campground and visitor center. Water and restrooms are available at the campground but not at the trailhead.

Description

The trail follows an old dirt road east along Islay Canyon, about 60 feet above the bed of Islay Creek. The canyon is thickly vegetated, with willow trees, oaks and a great variety of vines and shrubs forming a solid wall of greenery along the water.

The trail is nearly level, following an almost imperceptible grade as it heads upstream. This leg of the route is open to horses and bicyclists, both of which have the right of way over hikers, so be alert and move to the side if you encounter them.

At 2.1 miles the trail reaches a junction with the South Fork loop, which goes to the right and crosses Islay Creek. Stay on the road as the canyon narrows, crossing a trickle of water on a wooden bridge and passing an old barn at 2.8 miles. At 3 miles, turn left at a junction with the East Boundary Trail.

The narrow footpath climbs moderately steeply along a hillside covered with bush monkeyflower, reaching the crest of the ridge at 3.9 miles. The route continues uphill, following the ridge and offering good views back into Islay Canyon. At 4.1 miles the trail levels out and passes a stand holding shovels, rakes and other tools provided for volunteers maintaining the trail. The view from this spot is lovely, encompassing a broad stretch of coastline.

Now the trail descends, crossing an open, grassy hillside. It passes an outcropping of greenish-black serpentine, which forms an inhospitable soil when it weathers. Note how stunted and meager the grass is on the serpentine slope, compared with that growing elsewhere on the hillside.

The trail undulates for the next half-mile, and then climbs past a grove of oaks clinging to the side of the ridge. The route is mostly level beyond the grove until the trail reaches a junction at 5 miles with the Barranca Trail, which comes in from the left. Continue ahead, reaching a saddle and dropping at 5.3 miles to a junction with the Manzanita Trail, which goes to the right. Turn left and follow the Ridge Trail as it begins climbing toward Hazard Peak, at 1076 feet the highest point on the hike.

At 5.6 miles the trail reaches a junction with a spur that leads to the right to a knob with nice views of the coastline. Stay to the left and follow the crest of the ridge to the summit at 6.3 miles. The last few yards are rather steep, but the view is worth the effort. From the summit, the panorama includes Morro Bay, Point Sal, dunes and beaches, the rugged mountains of the Santa Lucia Range and the folded interior canyons and ridges of Montaña de Oro. There's even a bench where weary hikers can rest and enjoy the view.

From the summit, the trail follows the ridge line downhill, steeply at times, as it leads west. At 6.9 miles the trail drops off the crest of the ridge and begins a steeper descent, reaching an old marine terrace at 7.3 miles. The trail here is sandy, evidence that the terrace was once at sea level. You reach Pecho Valley Road at 7.9 miles; follow the road south to your starting point at 8 miles. ■

Hike #39: Morro Bay Sand Spit

Distance	10 miles
Level of difficulty	Moderate
Child rating	10 and up
Starting elevation	80 feet
Lowest point on trail	0 feet
Topographic map	Morro Bay South 7.5'
Guidebook maps	20 and 21

Few places on the California coast boast as wide a range of shoreline environments as the long sand spit that separates Morro Bay and its estuary from the waters of the Pacific Ocean. The rich set of ecosystems includes open beach, pounded by waves and scattered with the shells of near-shore mollusks and crustaceans; a complex system of dunes stabilized by delicate shrubs and grasses; and salt-marsh mudflats exposed at low tide on the bay side of the spit.

So fragile and unique is this collection of ecosystems that it has been granted special protection as the Morro Dunes Natural Preserve, a restricted area within Montaña de Oro and Morro Bay state parks. Travel through the dunes is prohibited except along certain corridors, to protect the delicate vegetation that keeps the sand from blowing away.

This hike to the end of the sand spit is a long one, and is best undertaken at low tide. At high tide, the part of the route that follows the bay side of the spit will be under water, depriving you of the chance to enjoy the views of the bay and the rich diversity of birds and mammals drawn by the still waters and the abundant food supply. Consult a tide table before setting out.

Beachcombers will love this walk, as will birders, who will have a chance to see dozens of species: endangered brown pelicans, great egrets, black-crowned night herons, great blue herons, sandpipers, whimbrels, curlews, cormorants. Turkey vultures are sometimes drawn to the shore to feed on the carcasses of dead sea lions and sea otters that wash up on the beach, and rare peregrine falcons nest in the nooks and crannies of Morro Rock, which juts up from the sea just across the boat channel from the end of the sand spit. In all, about 250 species of birds are permanent or seasonal residents of the area.

To reach the trailhead, follow Los Osos Valley Road and then Pecho Valley Road south toward the entrance to Montaña de Oro State Park. Turn right onto Sand Spit Road 0.7 mile south of the park boundary, and follow it a half-mile to the parking lot and picnic area at road's end. The picnic area offers restrooms and interpretive displays but no water. The hike begins on the boardwalk that leads west from the parking lot.

Description

The gray plastic boardwalk leads through the dunes to the beach at 0.4 mile. The dunes are particularly scenic in morning light, the low-angle rays of the sun casting their curves and ripple marks into high relief. Plant life includes sand verbena, beach primrose — notable for being pollinated exclusively by bumblebees — and buckwheat. The Morro Bay Sand Spit is one of the least disturbed coastal strands in California, and hence offers a chance to observe this unusual environment in something close to its natural state.

Upon reaching the beach, head for the packed sand at the surf line and turn right, heading north. Walking is much easier along the water's edge, and the hiker will be rewarded with a wealth of shells cast up by the waves. Among the most common are the delicate circular skeletons of sand dollars, a variety of sea urchin that while alive is covered by tiny flexible spines and tube feet. Also prominent among the litter are the heavy, handsome shells of the Pismo clam, which lives only on sandy beaches swept by heavy surf. Being filter feeders, most clams require still, clear water, but the Pismo has an ingenious internal screen that enables it to filter out the swirling sand as it draws water into its body to extract the microscopic bits of food it contains.

At 4 miles, the route crosses one of the breakwaters guarding the entrance to Morro Bay. Clamber over the rocks and continue on the other

Morro Rock seen (through the mist) from Morro Bay Sand Spit

side, following the waterline to a second breakwater at 4.5 miles. Morro Rock, a plug of erosion-resistant volcanic rock roughly 25 million years old, looms over the bay's entrance just across a narrow channel from the end of the sand spit, and this is a good place to rest awhile with a pair of binoculars to watch nesting birds flit about the landmark's rugged face.

Cross the second breakwater and continue along the edge of the spit, following the shore as it curves around to the east, then to the south. Across the bay are the towering stacks of a Pacific Gas & Electric Co. power plant, next to some of the commercial fishing docks of Morro Bay.

As you follow the shoreline south on the bay side of the spit, the environment changes from that of open beach to protected tidal mudflats. It is common to see a wide variety of birds probing the mud for food, or bobbing in the calm waters just beyond. Sea otters and sea lions also enjoy the shelter of the bay, and often may be seen swimming near the shore.

At 6.2 miles the shoreline curves to the west, angling toward a particularly high sand dune. Continue west at this point, cut through the dunes and return to the beach. Be careful to stay in the sandy hollows and avoid trampling the fragile vegetation. Slogging through the soft sand is tiring, but it offers a chance to examine the dunes at close range. As a bonus, keep an eye out for thick deposits of shell fragments in the protected hollows between the dunes. These represent the centuries-old trash heaps of seasonal Chumash camps.

Your path reaches the beach again at 6.5 miles. Turn left, head south along the sand spit to the boardwalk and follow it to the parking area and your starting point, at 10 miles.   ■

Hike #40: Oats Peak

Distance	7.5 miles
Level of difficulty	Moderate
Child rating	10 and up
Starting elevation	40 feet
Highest point on trail	1373 feet
Topographic maps	Morro Bay South, Port San Luis 7.5'
Guidebook map	21

This loop hike samples a representative selection of nearly all the park's major landforms and ecosystems, climbing from the banks of Islay Creek to the summit of the park's second-highest peak, dropping into a lush, creek-watered canyon and ending on the bluffs overlooking the surf. Along the way, the trail passes through thick chaparral, wildflower-strewn meadows, groves of gnarled oak trees and open grassland on an old marine terrace.

The trailhead is on the south side of the road into the main campground, across from the visitor center and adjacent to a maintenance building and parking area. A sign identifies it as the start of the Reservoir Flats Trail.

Description

The trail climbs immediately, crossing a hillside of chaparral — the thick, drought-resistant assemblage of woody shrubs that is typical of warm, dry slopes in the coastal mountains of Central and Southern California. The tread is rocky and broad as it works its way along the slope above the campground.

Good ocean views open up almost immediately during the moderate initial ascent. At 0.2 mile the trail forks; to the left lies the Reservoir Flats Trail. Bear right, continuing to climb through thick brush. Poison oak, bush lupine and ferns join the plant community, which reaches more than head-high. At 0.5 mile the trail reaches another junction. To the right is a path leading to the summit of Valencia Peak. Stay to the left and continue the steady climb.

At 1 mile the trail crosses a trickle of water running from a nearby spring. There's a concrete catch-basin to the right of the trail, and the moisture supports a lush growth of water-loving plants, including willow trees. Beyond the stream the trail grows steeper, climbing jumbo steps created by timbers embedded in the trail to slow erosion.

At 1.5 miles the trail reaches a low saddle between Oats and Valencia peaks, where the brush gives way to grasses and wildflowers in season, including poppies, lupine, blue dicks and monkeyflowers. There is a junction here with the other end of the Valencia Peak trail, which leads to the right. Views of the peak from here reveal the great beds of contorted sandstone that form its bulk. Careful examination of the slope reveals the presence of several terraces, which mark old shorelines elevated high above the sea by the immense pressures of tectonic collision. Follow the Oats Peak trail to the left. Below and to the south, hikers can peer down into the steep Coon Creek drainage.

The trail continues to climb, crossing an old fence line and following the ridge toward the summit of Oats Peak, which it reaches at 2.7 miles. The 360-degree view includes Morro Rock and Morro Bay to the north, and on a clear day reaches all the way to Point Piedras Blancas on the coast north of San Simeon. Views inland reveal the jumbled topography of the Sierra Madre.

Just beyond the summit, identified by a U.S. Geodetic Survey marker, the trail forks again. A faint and unmaintained track leads to the left toward the summit of Alan Peak, the highest in the park. Turn right and follow the descending trail as it leads into the Coon Creek drainage across hillsides densely covered with brush. The south-facing slopes have a slightly different community of plants, including thick oak trees and showy ceanothus, a woody shrub approaching tree height, which bears striking blue flowers attractive to bees. Poison oak also appears to prefer this side of the mountain, growing in enormous stands that intrude alarmingly into the path.

The trail switchbacks as it descends, reaching the floor of Coon Canyon in a large grove of immense canyon oaks at 3.6 miles. Turn right at the trail junction; to the left is a short track that dead-ends just upstream.

From here the trail leads through a thickly vegetated riparian corridor along Coon Creek, which may be heard but not often seen as it trickles through the thick undergrowth. Willows, big-leaf maples and black cottonwoods form a shady roof overhead, and the trail is mostly level as it follows the gently winding course of the creek. After crossing several bridges, the trail reaches a junction at 4.5 miles with a pack trail that goes off to the right and climbs the wall of the canyon. Continue straight ahead, following the canyon to its mouth.

At 5.3 miles the trail climbs over a small ridge, then descends into a gully and climbs back out, reaching the parking area at the Coon Canyon trailhead at 5.5 miles. Cross the parking area and Pecho Valley Road, picking up the trail again on the west side of the pavement.

From here the trail leads across a broad marine terrace worn level by wave action when the land lay at sea level. The vegetation growing from the sandy, salty soil is markedly different from that on the mountain slopes to the east, consisting primarily of tough grasses and hardy New Zealand spinach, an imported succulent with thick, fleshy leaves that resembles ice plant. The trail is level the rest of the way, leading to the edge of cliffs and roughly paralleling the shoreline before returning to the campground entrance. Side trails are crossed at quarter-miles intervals, each leading back to the park road.

It is dangerous to approach the edge of the bluffs, which are crumbling and eroded, and rise as much as 40 feet above the water. Signs warn of the hazard and advise staying back. It is imperative that hikers with children keep them under control.

The view from the trail is spectacular; crashing surf competes for attention with a rich variety of bird and marine life. Avian visitors include cormorants, gulls, pelicans and albatrosses, and pigeon guillemots build nests in holes on the cliff face. In the water below, harbor seals and sea otters cavort, while in the distance the spouts of migrating gray whales may be seen during the winter and early spring as they travel their long path between Alaska and the lagoons of Baja California.

The trail turns away from the bluffs at a point overlooking Corallina Cove at 7 miles. Follow it back toward the park road, passing a bridge and a pair of outhouses at 7.1 miles. The trail meets the park road at a pullout about 100 yards south of the campground entrance. Follow the road back to your starting point, at 7.5 miles. ■

**Oak grove along
Oats Peak trail**

Hike #41: Reservoir Flats

Distance	1.7 miles
Level of difficulty	Easy
Child rating	5 and up
Starting elevation	80 feet
Highest point on trail	320 feet
Topographic map	Morro Bay South 7.5′
Guidebook map	21

A good introduction to the range of plant life and topography in the Montaña de Oro area, the Reservoir Flats trail leads along a riparian corridor lush with moisture-loving vegetation, climbs over a sage-scrub hillside and visits the site of a water supply developed during the property's ranching days.

The trailhead is at the east end of the park campground, next to site #40. Day-use parking is not allowed in the campground, so unless you are staying overnight you must park at the visitor center and walk to the trailhead. This will add about half a mile to the round-trip distance.

Description

The trail undulates as it follows the course of Islay Creek up the canyon from the campground. Broad and well-used, the path clings to the side of the ridge, which is clad with a dense growth of blackberries, willows, oaks, wild cucumber, poison oak, vetch and horehound. At some points, the lichen-draped trees hang over the trail from both sides, creating a leafy tunnel.

At 0.7 mile the trail reaches a junction. Turn right and climb out of the shady streamside corridor onto a sunny hillside covered by sage scrub. At 0.8 mile the trail offers good views back down into Islay Canyon.

The climb grows more moderate at 0.9 mile as the trail reaches a saddle atop the ridge. Poppies, bush monkeyflower, coyote brush and black mustard cover the hillside, as the trail continues its gentle climb, offering views of the ocean to the west and the upper end of the campground to the north.

At 1.2 miles the trail reaches its highest point and begins descending to Reservoir Flats, a bowl caught between two ridges, where moisture supports a dense growth of tall grass. The trail skirts the former reservoir site at 1.4 miles and turns southwest, becoming broad and rocky. At 1.5 miles the trail meets the Oats Peak Trail, which leads to the left toward one of the park's notable summits. Turn right, descending sharply at times, and continue to the campground road near the visitor center at 1.7 miles. ■

Guadalupe-Nipomo Dunes Preserve

(See map on page 108)

Geological History

Stretching for more than 18 miles along California's Central Coast, the Nipomo Dunes are the second-largest dunes complex in California and include the largest dune in the western United States: Mussel Rock Dune, reaching a height of 500 feet.

The preserve is much more than just a sea of sand. A 1980 report by the Department of the Interior called the dunes as "the most unique and fragile ecosystem in the state of California." Along with 18 square miles of dunes, some of them thousands of years old, the preserve contains unusual coastal wetlands, including a dozen freshwater lakes impounded by the creeping sand. In this strange blend of fresh and salt water, sand and soil, live a startling variety of plants and animals, some of them found nowhere else.

The dunes trace their origin back 18,000 years, to the last glacial period. It was a time of fierce winds and unsettled weather, and the great volume of sediment eroded off the Santa Lucia Mountains to the north was dumped into the Pacific by the swollen Santa Maria River and dozens of smaller streams. Currents carried the debris south, to where the curving coastline between Point Sal and Point San Luis caught and trapped it. The sediments washed up onto the beach, where the particles were battered and broken and polished by waves. Once they'd been worn small enough by the surf, those sand grains rode the storm winds inland, a stinging cloud that settled wherever it encountered an obstruction.

Once forming a sandspit enclosing a bay, probably appearing much as Morro Bay does today, the moving dunes eventually filled in the open water and choked off the creeks that fed it, forming small freshwater lakes trapped between lobes of sand. Over thousand of years, vegetation took hold in the sand, stabilizing it and trapping even more flying debris in roots and stems. The dunes grew in height and ceased their inland migration. The oldest dunes are on top of the Nipomo and Orcutt mesas east of the preserve. The youngest, formed within the past 10,000 years, are those between the mesas and the beach.

Stability is tenuous. Anything that damages the dunes vegetation — off-road vehicles, trampling, clearing for homes and farms — frees the sand to move again, as farmers and homeowners on the edge of the dunes complex have learned to their dismay.

Human History

Chumash lived and hunted in the dunes as long as 8,000 years ago, subsisting primarily on a diet of seafood. Their trash heaps, filled with discarded shell fragments, may be found buried in the sand throughout the preserve. These camps were probably seasonal, for although fresh water was abundant, the dunes offered little in the way of shelter or raw materials with which to construct it.

The dunes weren't explored by Europeans until 1769, when Gaspar de Portolá's expedition camped and traveled through them while searching for an overland route between San Diego and Monterey. One of their campsites was at a lake they named "Oso Flaco," meaning "skinny bear," for the condition of the underfed grizzly they shot there.

After the Civil War, Americans purchased the dunes and surrounding property for ranching and farming. The dunes drew attention from other quarters, as well: Photographers Ansel Adams and Edward Weston found the sand a captivating subject; filmmaker Cecil B. DeMille built massive sets for his silent 1923 epic *The Ten Commandments* on the dunes south of the Santa Maria River and shot key scenes there (the sets were buried and left in place after filming); a group of intellectual dreamers called the Dunites established a utopian community there in the 1930s; and during World War II, poles were placed in bunkers along the shoreline to simulate cannons and discourage a potential Japanese invasion.

In the 1960s, the dunes drew a different kind of attention when Pacific Gas & Electric Co. purchased property there for a nuclear power plant. Local preservationists persuaded PG&E that the dunes were more valuable in their natural state, and the company decided to build farther north, at a remote and almost inaccessible location known as Diablo Canyon.

Land within the Nipomo Dunes complex is owned today by a checker-board of interests: oil companies, the state of California, private landowners, and Santa Barbara and San Luis Obispo counties. The Nature Conservancy, a private, non-profit conservation organization, has brought the many owners together in an attempt to coordinate preservation and management efforts. Guadalupe-Nipomo Dunes Preserve, at 3,417 acres, protects a small but significant part of the 18-square-mile dunes complex.

It is managed cooperatively by The Nature Conservancy and the state, which acquired most of the property in 1982.

By 1982, unrestricted off-road vehicle traffic had all but destroyed the dunes ecosystem. The preserve was closed to such use when it came under state ownership, and a painstaking process of revegetation and restoration has transformed the nearly lifeless expanse of sand into an ecological treasure.

Plants and Animals

Dunes constitute a harsh environment — dry, unstable, saline and beset by sandblasting winds carrying sharp-edged grains of quartz. Those plants that do thrive in the dunes are generally salt-tolerant, drought-resistant, low-growing and leathery. The Nipomo Dunes contain a particularly rich and interesting variety of plants, in part because of their location: Located at about the midpoint of the coastline between San Francisco and Los Angeles, they straddle a dividing line where plants at the northernmost extent of their range overlap with other plants at the southernmost extent of their own range.

Because of its unusual combination of fresh-water lakes, brackish estuaries, creeks and sand dunes, it is also home to plants found nowhere else. At least 18 species of rare or endangered plants grow in the dunes, including the la graciosa thistle, surf thistle, beach spectacle pod, dune Indian paintbrush and crisp dune mint. One plant, the Nipomo Mesa lupine, is represented by only a handful of individuals.

Among the preserve's animal inhabitants are raccoons and coyotes, while more than 200 bird species live in or migrate through it. Among them are such rarities as the California least tern and the brown pelican, both endangered, and the snowy plover and the black-shouldered kite.

Access

There are three entrances to the Guadalupe-Nipomo Dunes Preserve. The first is the West Main Street entrance just south of Guadalupe, leading to the southern half of the preserve. This provides the best access for visitors interested in the location where *The Ten Commandments* was filmed or who want to hike to Mussel Rock Dune, the tallest in the West. From State Highway 1, turn west on Highway 166 (West Main Street) in the town of Guadalupe and follow it 5 miles through the entrance gate to the free parking lot.

The second entrance is 3.8 miles north of Guadalupe and leads to Oso Flaco Lake. Turn west off Highway 1 on Oso Flaco Lake Road and follow it 3 miles to the dirt parking lot cooperatively managed by The Nature Conservancy and the state.

The third offers access to the north part of the complex, the Pismo Dunes. Follow Highway 1 to the small town of Oceano and turn west on Pier Avenue. Park in the lot at the end of the street and walk south past the mouth of Arroyo Grande Creek.

Visitor Centers

There aren't any visitor centers — yet. The Nature Conservancy is developing plant and animal checklists and other materials, offers a modest selection of docent-led nature hikes, and plans to build an interpretive center. Until then, all you can do is direct your questions to the volunteer or ranger on duty at the Oso Flaco Lake entrance kiosk.

Campgrounds

No camping is allowed in the preserve. There are campgrounds to the north at Pismo State Beach and Oceano Memorial County Park. Travelers with motorhomes can also find space at Pismo Coast Village RV Resort.

Food, Gas and Lodging

There are no services in the preserve. There are plenty of motels, stores and gas stations in the area, however, particularly in the towns of Pismo Beach and Grover City. Arroyo Grande and Santa Maria, good-sized towns located a bit farther inland on Highway 101, are also good bets for those seeking overnight accommodations. While Guadalupe is conveniently close, it is a tiny town of farm workers; it has some interesting restaurants and markets but not much in the way of lodging.

Phone Numbers and Addresses

For more information about Guadalupe-Nipomo Dunes Preserve, or to reserve space on a docent-led nature walk, call (805) 545-9925 or (805) 546-8378, or write to: Public Use Program Manager, Guadalupe-Nipomo Dunes Preserve, P.O. Box 15810, San Luis Obispo, CA 93406

For more information about The Nature Conservancy, call (415) 777-0487. To make camping reservations at the state beach parks in the Pismo area, call DESTINET at (800) 444-7275.   ∎

Trails of Guadalupe-Nipomo Dunes Preserve

There is only one formal trail in the Nipomo Dunes, a 2.2-mile round-trip excursion over bridge and boardwalk across Oso Flaco Lake to the beach. There are other opportunities for exploration, however, if you are willing to walk along the beach.

On the north, the Pismo Dunes Preserve is accessible from the town of Oceano, offering miles of open sand to explore at will. From the Oso Flaco Lake entrance, hikers can explore the central part of the dunes, including Coreopsis Hill and the Mobil Coastal Preserve, neither of which is marked but both of which are to the south of the boardwalk's end. From the West Main Street entrance south of Guadalupe, hikers can gain access to the Mussel Rock Dune area.

Hiking in sand is tiring. Be sure to wear high-top shoes to keep out the grit, and bring a hat and sunscreen — there is no shade in the dunes. Morning is the best time to hike, especially on sunny days, for the low-angle light highlights the golden color of the sand, and the tracks left the night before by insects and other creatures will still be undisturbed

The coast can be quite windy, so pack a sweater if you plan to be out in the afternoon. Pack plenty of water, too, for you will find none in the preserve. ■

Hike #42: Oso Flaco Lake

Distance	2.2 miles
Level of difficulty	Easy
Child rating	5 and up
Starting elevation	20 feet
Highest point on trail	30 feet
Topographic map	Oceano 7.5′
Guidebook map	22

Less a hike than a casual stroll, this trail — part of it through sand, much of it over a wooden boardwalk designed to minimize damage to the fragile and rare plant life of the Nipomo Dunes — leads visitors through a landscape unlike that anywhere else in California. A fresh-water lake and sluggish creek support a rich array of plants, many of them rare, surrounded by a vast expanse of golden sand washed by the sea

The trailhead is at the dirt parking area at the end of Oso Flaco Lake Road, near the entrance kiosk where a staff member, either a volunteer with The Nature Conservancy or a ranger for the California Department of Parks and Recreation, will collect the $4 fee and provide information about the preserve. Restrooms are provided but no water is available at the trailhead.

Description

The trail follows a paved road through a thick, shady stand of trees to the shore of Oso Flaco Lake at 0.2 mile. Here the path goes to the left, onto a bridge that makes a jog about midway across the water and deposits you on the west shore of the lake. The bridge is a great place to watch birds, which abound in the water and along the lake's reedy shoreline. Among those commonly seen are coots, mallards, loons, pintails, ruddy ducks and widgeons. Raccoons may sometimes be seen foraging even in daylight in the thick reeds at the edge of the lake, where they hunt for crustaceans and amphibians.

The bridge ends at 0.4 miles. The boardwalk continues from the bridge through the dunes, past stands of blue and yellow bush lupine and other scrub plants. From the boardwalk, you can look to the northeast and see the edge of the preserve, the boundary made clear by the sudden end of all vegetation where the popular Oceano Dunes State Vehicular Recreation Area begins. The recreation area has been turned into a sandy moonscape by off-road vehicle use, which destroys the stabilizing plant life and allows the dunes to migrate inland.

Walking off the boardwalk is prohibited within the preserve, except along the beach, both to protect the fragile vegetation — much of it replanted recently by The Nature Conservancy in an effort to stabilize the dunes and restore the original ecosystem — and to prevent hikers from disturbing nesting birds. The endangered least tern, among other rare species, lays its eggs in the dunes, where they are easily trampled.

At 0.9 mile the trail splits, a short path leading to the left through sand and over a dune with nice views of the preserve and the sea. The boardwalk continues to the right and ends on the beach at 1.1 miles. It's possible to walk about 50 yards south from the boardwalk's end and pick up the other fork of the trail on the way back. There's a bench at the junction, although it's even more pleasant to continue on and find a seat on the beach, where the views encompass many miles of coastline.

After a suitable interval of basking and frolicking in the surf, return the way you came.   ■

Boardwalk trail and lupines at Nipomo Dunes

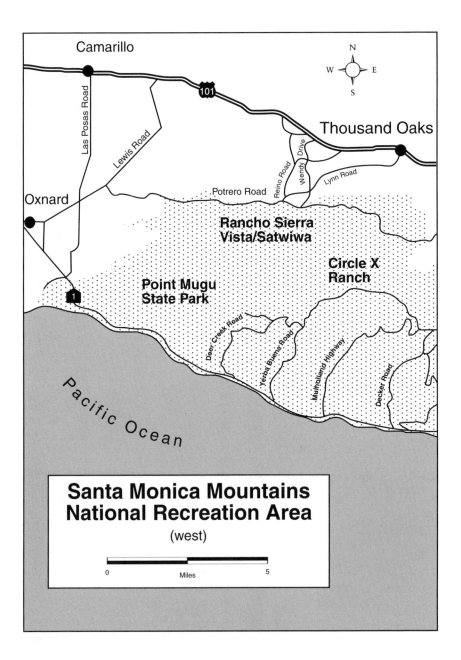

Camarillo

N
W ⟡ E
S

Las Posas Road

Lewis Road

101

Thousand Oaks

Reino Road

Wendy Drive

Lynn Road

Potrero Road

Oxnard

Rancho Sierra
Vista/Satwiwa

Circle X
Ranch

Point Mugu
State Park

Deer Creek Road

Yerba Buena Road

Mulholland Highway

Decker Road

1

Pacific Ocean

Santa Monica Mountains
National Recreation Area
(west)

0   Miles   5

Santa Monica Mountains National Recreation Area

Geological History

Unlike most of California's mountain ranges, which have a generally north-south orientation, the Santa Monicas run east-west. They are part of a geographic province known as the Transverse Ranges, in recognition of their odd, crosswise trend. In addition to the Santa Monica range, the province includes the Santa Ynez Mountains of Santa Barbara and Ventura counties, and the San Gabriel and San Bernardino mountains of Los Angeles and San Bernardino counties.

Examination of a map of California offers a clue to this puzzlingly perpendicular orientation. The coastline makes a great bend at the west end of the Transverse Ranges. The curve is matched by a corresponding kink in the San Andreas Fault system, which marks the boundary of two moving slabs of the Earth's crust, the Pacific Plate and the North American Plate. The Pacific Plate, which lies under the ocean but is also carrying a slice of coastal California on its back, is sliding north relative to the motion of the North American Plate.

Along most of the border, the two plates grind past each other in fits and starts, producing earthquakes. But at the bend, the north-moving Pacific Plate has become hung up on the protruding edge of the North American Plate. Instead of sliding past its neighbor, the Pacific Plate is crunching into it. The force of the collision has compressed and crumpled the landscape, creating the Santa Monica Mountains and the other Transverse Ranges.

The rocks of which the Santa Monicas are formed are primarily old sea sediments, mostly Miocene in age, dating back about 25 million years. They include a variety of sandstones, mudstones and shale, indicating they were deposited near the shore. Many of the layers contain abundant fossils of clams, snails and other shellfish, which are exposed in the stream-cut canyons.

The sedimentary rocks, which have been lifted and folded, are intruded by volcanic rocks, especially in the mountains' interior. These 16-million-

145

year-old volcanics form the erosion-resistant summits of the highest peaks in the Santa Monicas, including Boney Mountain and misnamed Sandstone Peak.

The period of mountain building that raised the Santa Monicas to their current height began about 10 million years ago, making the range rather young in geological terms. The rapid uplift has produced steep and rugged terrain, because erosion has had relatively little time to soften the contours of the slopes.

Human History

Because the region is dry and rugged, human use of the Santa Monica Mountains began rather late in California prehistory, commencing about 7,500 years ago. In the west part of the range, the part on which this book focuses, ancestors of the modern Chumash began establishing hunting camps in the interior valleys, while on the coast they built large villages. These were typically located on the plain near the mouths of perennial streams, and evidence of large, permanent settlements has been found at Malibu Canyon, Point Dume, Big and Little Sycamore canyons and La Jolla Valley.

Plant food, such as seeds (sage and grass), berries (toyon and hollyleaf cherry) and nuts (California walnut) constituted the mainstay of their diet, although shellfish gradually became more important along the coast, and acorns — which required the development of special technology to remove the bitter, toxic tannin they contain, and were therefore not consumed by the earliest inhabitants — became more prominent among inland residents.

By the time the Chumash culture had developed, about 1,500 years ago, the shift to a marine-based subsistence, augmented by acorns collected from inland oak groves, was complete. The population expanded, and coastal villages grew large, establishing outposts in the interior valleys for hunting and acorn gathering. They also established trading networks with their neighbors.

East of Malibu Canyon, the Santa Monica Mountains were home to people whose language belonged to the Shoshonean family, a common language family shared by native cultures throughout the American Southwest and the Great Basin region of Nevada and Utah. Aside from language, the natives living east of Malibu were much like the Chumash in their technology and subsistence patterns.

Europeans arrived in this part of California in 1542, when Spanish explorer Juan Cabrillo sailed through the Santa Barbara Channel and became the first outsider to report seeing the Santa Monica Mountains. Other seafarers passed along the coast, but not until 1769 did explorers travel through the mountains themselves.

Gaspar de Portolá was the first, leading his expedition through the region in 1769 while seeking to establish an overland route between Spanish settlements at San Diego and at Monterey. Traveling north, his party reached the mountains in August of that year, followed Sepulveda Pass (crossed today by Interstate 405), into the San Fernando Valley and then followed the Santa Clara River from Castaic to the coast at what is now Oxnard. They then continued north.

On their return trip along the coast, they headed inland from the Oxnard Plain and entered the mountains, crossing by way of Cahuenga Pass on an old Indian trail (the route followed today by Highway 101 near Hollywood).

The Portolá expedition was followed in short order by the Franciscan missionaries, who established permanent missions — each a combination of military outpost and religious center — at San Fernando and Ventura. No Spanish settlements were built in the Santa Monicas themselves, but the natives who lived there found themselves forced to abandon their traditional ways and traditional village sites as Spanish soldiers enforced the missionaries' wish to have the natives close at hand. Forcibly converted to Christianity and put to work growing food and maintaining the mission settlements, the Chumash began to lose their culture and their language. Foreign diseases and bad diet caused the mortality rate to soar.

The vast and rugged Santa Monica Mountains afforded some protection for those Chumash who sought haven in its canyons, far from the "civilizing" influence of the padres. That haven was short-lived. In the 1830s, the Mexican government ordered the breakup of the mission system and the transfer of its land holdings to private owners. The Santa Monica Mountains were divided among several enormous ranchos. Two of them — Rancho Guadalasca and Rancho Topanga-Malibu-Sequit — encompassed nearly the entire west half of the mountains, and sent great herds of Mexican longhorn cattle into the valleys to graze.

The ranchos were broken up following Mexico's defeat in the Mexican-American War and California's 1850 statehood. Lacking significant mineral deposits, the Santa Monicas continued to be used primarily for ranching until the turn of the century, when urban Los Angeles begin pushing up into the eastern canyons and ridges. Many ranches were subdivided into home lots, and wealthy businessmen and Hollywood stars bought vast tracts of mountain land as an investment.

As the population of Southern California grew, the rugged Santa Monica Mountains acquired value for their wild, open qualities — amenities that were increasingly in short supply in the region. Aided by donations of land by individuals and private organizations, local and state agencies established parks to preserve some of the most spectacular features: the beaches and some of the canyons and scenic ridges.

In 1978, Congress formalized the patchwork of local and state parks by creating the 70,000-acre Santa Monica Mountains National Recreation Area, a sprawling jigsaw puzzle of protected land adjacent to one of the most populated regions in the country. Stretching from Point Mugu State Park on the west to Griffith Park on edge of downtown Los Angeles on the east, the Santa Monica Mountains NRA includes 15 state beaches and dozens of city, state and county parks. Administration of this tangle of public recreation sites is complicated further by the existence of private-public agencies formed solely to acquire additional land for inclusion in the park.

Ten miles wide and 50 miles long, the recreation area is within a one-hour drive of 10 million people, constituting one of the most remarkable expanses of near-urban wilderness in the country.

The area of most interest to readers of this book is that part within Ventura County, comprising primarily Point Mugu State Park, Circle X Ranch and Rancho Sierra Vista/Satwiwa. The first is administered by the state; the latter two are property of the National Park Service, which has overall authority over the National Recreation Area.

Plants and Animals

The Santa Monica Mountains are characterized by nine different plant communities: kelp beds off the shore, beaches, the salt marshes at Malibu and Mugu lagoons, the coastal sage scrub and the chaparral blanketing the hillsides, the oak woodlands and the grasslands of broad valleys, and freshwater marshes and riparian woodlands along perennial streams.

By far the most widespread of these are the coastal sage scrub and chaparral communities. Both are adapted to hot, dry conditions and both rely on periodic wildfires to clear them of old brush and allow new growth to germinate.

Sage scrub, found typically on west-facing slopes above the beaches, includes such plants as coastal sagebrush, California buckwheat, lupine, bush monkeyflower and deer weed. Chaparral predominates on inland slopes and ridges, and includes a denser, woodier plant assemblage: chamise, toyon, laurel sumac, manzanita, ceanothus and scrub oak.

Notable examples of riparian woodland are found along La Jolla Canyon in Point Mugu State Park, which also preserves the largest native grassland in the mountains.

A similarly wide variety of creatures call the mountains home. Golden eagles and several species of hawks cruise the peaks and ridge crests, while gulls and brown pelicans frequent the beaches. Southern mule deer, coyotes and rabbits are commonly seen, and the park is also home to more reclusive animals: gray foxes, striped and spotted skunks, badgers, bobcats and mountain lions. It boasts a full complement of reptiles, including whiptail lizards, western fence lizards and several species of snakes. The one visitors are most likely to be concerned about is the southern Pacific rattlesnake, which is fairly common but seldom seen. Although it is venomous, it is eager to avoid confrontation and will usually vanish as soon as it senses the vibration of an approaching hiker.

The mountains also harbor two other unpleasant natives: poison oak and ticks. Poison oak is ubiquitous in the coastal mountains of California, and the prudent hiker learns to identify and avoid it. Just the same, it is a good idea to wash exposed skin with a strong soap after an outing in the Santa Monica Mountains, to strip away the irritating oil carried in the plant's leaves and stems.

Ticks are fairly common in brushy areas, and can carry disease. Long pants and sleeves are a good idea when traveling through dense under-growth, and a post-hike tick check is imperative. For additional informa-tion about dealing with ticks, snake bites, poison oak and other hazards of wilderness travel, see the list of recommended reading at the end of the book.

Access

There are literally hundreds of different ways to enter the Santa Monica Mountains National Recreation Area. For the areas described in this guide, however, the primary routes are by the Pacific Coast Highway, also known as State Highway 1, which runs along the coastline from Santa Monica to Oxnard, and the Highway 101 freeway, a major state route that runs along the inland border of the recreation area between Los Angeles and Ventura.

The best maps of trails and road access to the parkland are the series published by Tom Harrison Cartography in San Rafael, Calif. (1-800-265-9090). The company publishes two for this area: *Trail Map of the Santa Monica Mountains West* and *Trail Map of the Santa Monica Mountains East*. They're available at the park's visitor centers. An Automobile Club map of Ventura County is also useful for identifying the local streets leading to trailheads.

Visitor Centers

The Park Service operates an information center at its Santa Monica Mountains headquarters in Agoura Hills, as well as at Rancho Sierra Vista/ Satwiwa. Both stock some books and maps, the best selection being at park headquarters. The Satwiwa center doubles as a museum of Chumash culture.

The headquarters and the information center are open 8 A.M. to 5 P.M. Monday through Friday and 9 A.M. to 5 P.M. Saturday and Sunday. The center is open year-round except on Christmas, Thanksgiving and New Year's Day. The Satwiwa center is open only on Sundays, 10 A.M. to 5 P.M.

Information about hiking and camping is also available at the Circle X Ranch ranger station, but only when the ranger is not out on patrol. The station does not have regular public hours, but visitors are welcome to drop in if it is open.

Campgrounds

In the Ventura County part of the national recreation area, campgrounds are available in Point Mugu State Park and at Circle X Ranch.

The largest is Sycamore Canyon Campground, situated off Highway 1 in the state park. It has 55 sites with picnic tables and wood- or charcoal-burning stoves. Restrooms, drinking water and solar-heated showers are provided. The fee is $18 a night on Friday and Saturday, and $17 Sunday through Thursday. It has no hookups for recreational vehicles, but does have a trailer dump station. Sites can be reserved.

There is also a walk-in campground at La Jolla Valley, 2 miles by trail from the La Jolla Canyon trailhead on Highway 1 and 5 miles from the Sycamore Canyon Campground trailhead. It has several primitive sites with a capacity of 20 people; water and restrooms are available. The fee is $3 a night. Fires are prohibited. Sites are available on a first-come, first-served basis; campers check in at the La Jolla Canyon trailhead.

If you wish to camp near the surf, Point Mugu State Park also operates a campground at Thornhill Broome Beach, on Highway 1 across from the entrance to La Jolla Canyon. It has 63 sites, with water and restrooms, picnic tables and stoves. The fee is $14 a night on Friday and Saturday, and $11 Sunday through Thursday. Spaces can accommodate recreational vehicles and trailers up to 31 feet long, but there are no hookups and the nearest dump station is at Sycamore Canyon Campground. Sites can be reserved.

For groups, three large reservation-only sites are available in Point Mugu State Park: the group walk-in campground at La Jolla Valley, which can accommodate 25 people; the Danielson Multi-Use Area, which has space for up to 75 people and their horses, and has a barbecue pit, tables, restrooms, showers, electrical outlets and a fireplace; and the Sycamore Multi-Use Area, which can accommodate up to 40 people and their horses, and has tables, fire pits, restrooms, water, a pipe corral and a watering trough.

The fees for the group camps vary. Reservations are required and may be made up to six months in advance.

There are two campgrounds at Circle X Ranch. The group camp is just off Yerba Buena Road near the ranger station, and can accommodate up to 75 people. It has picnic tables, barbecue grills, restrooms and water, and reservations are required. Wood fires are prohibited. The fee is $2 per person per night.

Happy Hollow Campground, at the end of Happy Hollow Road a little over a mile south of the Circle X ranger station, has 18 tent-camping sites with picnic tables and barbecue grills. Restrooms and water are provided. Trailers and motorhomes are prohibited, as are wood fires. The fee is $6 a night, and sites are available on a first-come, first-served basis.

Food, Gas and Lodging

Services are available in the nearby communities of Oxnard and Thousand Oaks.

Phone Numbers and Addresses

For general information about the Santa Monica Mountains National Recreation Area, contact headquarters at (818) 597-1036. Address mailed inquiries to 30401 Agoura Road, Suite 100, Agoura Hills, CA 91301.

For information about Point Mugu State Park, contact the California Department of Parks and Recreation at (818) 880-0350 or write to 1925 Las Virgenes Road, Calabasas, CA 91302.

To reserve individual and family campsites at Point Mugu State Park, call the DESTINET reservation system at (800) 444-7275. To reserve group sites at the Danielson and Sycamore Multi-use sites in Point Mugu State Park, call (805) 488-5223. Additional information about the recreation area is available from the Santa Monica Mountains Conservancy at (310) 456-5046.

To inquire about demonstrations and other interpretive programs conducted at the Satwiwa Native American Indian Culture Center, call (805) 375-1930. ■

Trails of Santa Monica Mountains National Recreation Area

A word of caution: the USGS topographic maps of the Santa Monica Mountains are almost worthless for hiking, for two reasons. First, they are quite out of date, showing almost none of the campgrounds, roads and trails built in the past 30 years (and those improvements that have been mapped are often incorrect). The other reason is that the USGS cartographers, for reasons known only to themselves, decided to make the contour interval absurdly tiny on the maps of this region — 20 feet on some quads, 25 on others. This is about half the distance used on almost all other quads, and as a result there are twice as many contour lines as necessary on the maps depicting these mountains. The density of the lines makes the maps quite unreadable even with a magnifying glass.

A far better bet is to purchase one of the greatly superior sets of trail maps, complete with a reasonable amount of contour information, published by private firms. Best bets are *A Recreation Guide to Trails of the Santa Monica Mountains* by Canyon Publishing Co. in Canoga Park, and *Trail Map of the Santa Monica Mountains West* by Tom Harrison Cartography in San Rafael.

The trails described in the following pages are concentrated in three main areas: Point Mugu State Park, Rancho Sierra Vista and Circle X Ranch. These are just some of the dozens of individual parks and beaches making up the patchwork known as the Santa Monica Mountains National Recreation Area, but together they account for nearly all the public land in the Ventura County part of the NRA. The trails offer a sampling of all the attractions the park has to offer: rocky peaks, open grasslands, sycamore-shaded creeks and wildflower-strewn hillsides. ∎

Hike #43: The Grotto

Distance	3.5 miles
Level of difficulty	Easy
Child rating	5 and up
Starting elevation	1700 feet
Lowest point on trail	1200 feet
Topographic map	Triunfo Pass 7.5'
Guidebook map	23

This easy ramble down the West Fork Arroyo Sequit leads to a giant's playground of sheer cliffs and jumbled boulders where kids can spend hours exploring spooky "caves," clambering over ledges, splashing in the trickling stream and shouting to hear their voices echo down the canyon. The trip back is all uphill, though, so allow for that in deciding how long to play and how tired to let your children become before returning to your car.

The trailhead is at the Circle X Ranch ranger station, 5 miles up Yerba Buena Road from Highway 1. The turnoff from Highway 1 is about 9 miles east of Point Mugu and 1 mile west of the Los Angeles-Ventura County line. Park in the gravel lot at the station, where maps and information are available if the ranger is not out on patrol.

Description

Follow the dirt road downhill past the old ranch house to the group camping area. The road divides here at 0.2 mile, the right fork leading on to Happy Hollow Campground. Stay to the left, following the sign indicating the start of the Grotto Trail.

Continue through the group-camp parking area, past a fence and onto the trail, which leads through a brushy area alongside a creek shaded by large sycamores. Evidence of the 1993 Greenmeadow fire persists in the form of blackened trunks and charred debris on the ground, although most of the vegetation has long since recovered. At 0.3 mile the trail crosses the creek.

The trail continues downhill along the creek. At 0.5 mile the trail forks; bear right, cross the creek and climb away from the arroyo onto a grassy ridge. From the top, at 0.7 mile, there are nice views above and below, ranging from the deep canyon on the east to the picturesque rock formations of Sandstone Peak high on the slope to the north.

The trail descends on the other side of the ridge, steeply at times, and the footing is loose and rocky. At 1.1 miles the trail passes through a grove of coast live oaks, several of them killed by the fire. At 1.2 miles the path meets a dirt road near a picnic area with restrooms, tables, trash cans, a fireplace and water. Stay left at the junction, cross the flat along the creek and pick up the trail beyond the restrooms.

The trail parallels the creek and crosses its rocky bed at 1.4 miles, following the canyon past the walk-in campsites of Happy Hollow Campground. The trail forks; bear right (both branches rejoin just ahead, so it doesn't really matter, but the left-hand path climbs more). At 1.7 miles there is another junction, the right-hand track leading into the campground. Stay to the left, passing a sign NO CAMPING BEYOND THIS POINT and crossing the creek again.

The grotto lies about 100 yards downstream. It is shaded by California bay trees, which perfume the air with their aromatic scent. The sheer canyon walls are close together and rise high overhead; the canyon floor is choked with huge boulders jumbled together to form little caves and nooks. The cliffs and boulders are composed of volcanic breccia, a melange of rock fragments welded together into something that looks like chocolate-chip cookie dough. Through the rocks, the creek trickles and tumbles, forming small waterfalls and quiet pools. Some of the drops are fairly high, and small children bear watching so they don't take an ugly tumble.

Return the way you came. ■

Sandstone Peak, seen from the trail to the Grotto

Hike #44: La Jolla Canyon

Distance	7.5 miles
Level of difficulty	Moderate
Child rating	10 and up
Starting elevation	30 feet
Highest point on trail	1221 feet
Topographic map	Point Mugu 7.5′
Guidebook map	24

La Jolla (pronounced la HOY-a) Canyon contains one of the few perennial streams in these arid coastal mountains, supporting a rich community of riparian plants and animals. This loop trail also traverses one of the largest and best-preserved native grasslands in Southern California, climbs to windswept ridges with breathtaking views of the Pacific, and slips between eroded cliffs of fossil-bearing sandstone.

The trailhead is on the north side of Pacific Coast Highway, across the road from Thornhill Broome Beach Campground. There's a small parking area and signs identifying it as the Ray Miller Trailhead. The name honors a volunteer ranger who served as the first official campground host in the state park system and welcomed countless visitors to the park from his retirement in 1972 until his death in 1989.

It costs $6 to park in the lot. If that seems too steep, leave your car outside the park on the shoulder of Highway 1.

Walk to the locked gate at the north end of the parking lot. To your right is a sign indicating the Backbone Trail, your starting point. The Ray Miller Trailhead marks the western terminus of this remarkable trail, complete except for a couple of short segments. When all the links are in place, the trail will follow the "backbone" of the Santa Monica Mountains for 65 miles, linking the National Recreation Area's major state parks — Will Rogers, Topanga, Malibu Creek and Point Mugu.

Description

Follow the Backbone Trail across La Jolla Creek, climbing moderately across an open hillside of chamise, morning glory, yucca and grasses. The hillside was burned in 1989 but recovered quickly, as is typical of the chaparral plant community.

At 0.1 mile the trail intersects a horse path coming up from the new group campground below. Bear left and continue a steady, moderate ascent that, over the next mile, brings you ever-expanding views of the Santa Barbara Channel and its islands. Keep watch closer at hand for wildflowers, including poppies, blue dicks, mustard, shrubby butterweed and the lovely Mariposa lily.

At 1.2 miles the trail levels briefly on a promontory with great 180-degree views of the coastline. Then you resume the climb, leveling out finally at 2 miles as you cross a grassy area and attain the crest of the ridge. From here the trail undulates, following the ridge line and offering views of Boney Peak on the east and Laguna Peak on the west, the latter distinguished by the mass of radar domes and antennas bristling from the Navy installation on its summit.

At 2.8 miles the trail reaches a junction with the Overlook Trail. Turn left, following the broad track as it goes slightly uphill and then levels off to follow the contour of the ridge for the next mile.

At 4.1 miles the trail begins a descent to La Jolla Valley and its expansive grassland, visible below to the west. At 4.9 miles you reach a junction with a trail leading to the right and Sycamore Canyon. Stay to the left, reaching another junction at 5 miles where the Overlook Trail and the La Jolla Valley Loop Trail intersect. Turn left toward La Jolla Valley.

At 5.1 miles the trail splits again. Stay to the left and cross a broad meadow carpeted with rare native grasses. At 5.7 miles the trail passes a pond ringed by rushes and cattails, happily paddled by ducks and waded by herons. At 5.8 miles the trail intersects a connector leading to the La Jolla Valley walk-in campground on the right. Continue straight ahead and descend the wall of the canyon cut by La Jolla Creek, which can be seen through the oaks and sycamores on the right.

At 6.4 miles the Mugu Peak Trail branches off to the right. Go straight. The trail begins dropping steeply into the canyon at 6.7 miles, passing outcrops of fossil-bearing sedimentary rock and giant coreopsis plant. Also known as sea dahlia and tree sunflower, this striking plant features bright yellow flowers atop long stalks protruding from tufts of feath-

**Yucca flowers frame
Point Mugu**

Waterfall in La Jolla Canyon

ery leaves at the end of a thick, bulbous trunk. The overall effect is of a creation from the pages of a Dr. Seuss book. The giant coreopsis, which can reach 10 feet in height, blooms from March through May and is fairly uncommon.

At 7 miles you cross the creek next to a delicate waterfall that drops into a small pool shaded by trees and surrounded by large boulders, making a pleasant stopping place. At 7.1 miles, still descending, you cross the creek again, then level out and follow the canyon back to the trailhead at 7.5 miles. ■

Hike #45: Mugu Peak

Distance	5.5 miles
Level of difficulty	Moderate
Child rating	10 and up
Starting elevation	20 feet
Highest point on trail	1266 feet
Topographic map	Point Mugu 7.5'
Guidebook map	24

Fantastic views of the ocean, the Channel Islands and the Oxnard Plain await hikers who climb Mugu Peak, the westernmost summit of the Santa Monica Mountains open to the public. (Laguna Peak is farther west and 17 feet higher, but the Navy has a weather and communication installation on the summit, and military security discourages unannounced guests.) As a bonus, the trail crosses native grassland and follows a babbling creek, offering a sample of several interesting life zones.

Most guides would have hikers start their assault on Mugu Peak at the trailhead in La Jolla Canyon, making it an 11-mile round-trip. But if you're willing to scramble up a rough trail that pays little attention to grade, at least for the first mile, there's a shortcut.

The trailhead for this hike is on Highway 1 across the road from the orange observation tower at the shooting range on the Point Mugu military base, about 9 miles south of Oxnard. Pull into the small dirt parking area on the north side of the road.

Along several stretches, the trail winds through thick grass and brush. Long pants are advisable, making this a hike best done during cool weather.

Description

The trail climbs steeply from the parking area, heading up a rocky, steep ravine. It is well-used and easy to follow, but the grade is unrelenting. As a reward, the view is good almost immediately, encompassing the ocean, the military base and a complex of lagoons and wetlands.

At 0.5 mile the climb grows a little less steep, as the trail reaches a terrace covered with manzanita, sage and laurel sumac. The grade quickly resumes, however, abating somewhat when it reaches another terrace at 0.7 mile. At 0.9 mile you reach a junction with the Mugu Peak Trail, which wraps around the mountain. Go straight, crossing a saddle covered with grass and prickly pear cactus.

Beyond the saddle, the trail descends toward La Jolla Canyon, which is watered by a small creek that supports a corridor of oak and sycamore trees. The ground on this side of the mountain is thick with tall native grasses, and the trail is fainter. At 1.4 miles, there is a good, close-up view to the left of the Navy's communications facility atop Laguna Peak. At 1.5 miles the trail forks; bear right, following the signs indicating the La Jolla Loop Trail.

Level now, the trail continues through thick grass that can reach head high by late spring, making this a hike better undertaken in winter or early spring. At 2 miles you cross a creek flowing through a thick stand of oaks. Poison oak is abundant on the banks of the pleasant little stream, which would otherwise make a nice stopping place.

At 2.3 miles you reach a junction; bear right, and then right again at another junction about 100 yards beyond. The trail crosses the creek again and begins climbing the ridge on the other side. At 2.6 miles you reach the crest of the ridge, gaining views into a deep canyon below, and follow the ridge toward the base of the peak. At 3 miles you round a corner and begin heading west, parallel to the coast. The ascent is easy, and the views make all the sweat worthwhile.

At 3.3 miles, you reach a spur leading to the right. Follow it uphill, scrambling the final few yards to the summit, which you reach at 3.5 miles. A register and a flag mark the highest point, where the 360-degree view rewards you for all your effort.

Follow the spur back down to the main trail and turn right, contouring along the slope to rejoin the steep trail up from the parking area at 4.6 miles. Go left and retrace your steps to the parking area, which you reach at 5.5 miles. ■

Hike #46: Old Boney Trail

Distance	9.7 miles
Level of difficulty	Strenuous
Child rating	10 and up
Starting elevation	850 feet
Highest point on trail	1800 feet
Topographic map	Newbury Park 7.5'
Guidebook map	25

This lengthy semi-loop hike leads through the heart of Point Mugu State Park, traversing an official state wilderness area as it ranges between rolling grasslands, sycamore-shaded canyons and rugged mountain slopes. Although the climb is considerable, the grade is never excessive, and few hikes sample as many of the Santa Monica Mountains' ecosystems.

The trailhead is at the Rancho Sierra Vista/Satwiwa visitor center on the north side of the state park. To reach it, follow Highway 101 to the west end of Thousand Oaks and take the Borchard Road exit. Follow Borchard south of the freeway to Reino Road, turn left and go 2 miles to Potrero Road. Turn right and follow Potrero a short distance to the sign indicating the entrance to Rancho Sierra Vista/Satwiwa. Park in the visitor lot and follow the road to the visitor center. Water and restrooms are available.

Description

Follow the paved road south from the visitor center, through the locked gate. The road, which is closed to automobile traffic (except for official vehicles traveling to the ranger housing and other facilities in Big Sycamore Canyon) will serve as your route for the first 2.4 miles. Keep an eye out for bicyclists, crowds of whom whiz along the pavement on weekends.

The road leads across the rolling meadow south of the visitor center, past a fence line and a water tank, and drops steeply into Big Sycamore Canyon, shaded by its namesake trees. At 1.1 miles it reaches the bottom of the canyon and an intersection with the Fossil Trail coming in from the left. A portable toilet is usually stationed here.

Continue on the road, enjoying the deep shade and the profusion of birds and butterflies drawn by the thick tangle of vegetation in the creek bed, to a fork at 1.5 miles. Bear left, passing the Sycamore Multi-use Area, a campground and picnic area, and follow the signs to the Danielson Multi-Use Area, which is named after the last family to own this property.

The road reaches the old Danielson ranch house, now a park ranger residence, at 2.4 miles. Follow the dirt road past the house and the large barbecue pit in a shady grove of large oaks, to the start of the Backbone/

Blue Canyon Trail at 2.6 miles.

The narrow trail leads up the canyon into the Boney Mountain State Wilderness Area. Poison oak is lush along the stream, which is shaded by trees and runs late into the year. The trail crosses the gravelly bed and begins climbing up the north side of Blue Canyon, reaching a junction at 3.2 miles. Steer to the left and begin a moderately steep climb that leads for the next 2 miles along a ridge below the volcanic outcroppings of Boney Mountain itself.

The climb is not terribly steep but it is unceasing. Fortunately, there are good views across Big Sycamore Canyon and beyond Laguna Peak to the distant Oxnard Plain, as well as plenty of wildflowers on the brushy slope, to distract you from the task at hand. Chamise, bush monkeyflowers, canyon sunflowers and golden yarrow decorate the slope, drawing bees and hummingbirds.

At 5 miles the trail descends to a junction with the Fossil Trail, leading to the left. Stay to the right, resume the long ascent and regain the crest of the ridge at 5.2 miles. The views are spectacular now, reaching across the Conejo Valley to the mountains beyond. The climb continues to a junction at 5.8 miles, just below the reddish cliffs of Boney Mountain. Turn left, descending steeply at times as the trail begins returning you to the floor of Big Sycamore Canyon.

At 6.5 miles a trail to the right leads to an old cabin site. Little remains but a rock fireplace and chimney. Stay to the left and continue your descent into a small canyon, reaching a junction on the streambank at 7.2 miles. If you follow the path to the right, it leads upstream to some small cascades, which are popular with weekend visitors.

Head downstream, cross the creek at 7.4 miles and bear left at the junction just beyond. The trail follows the stream, crossing the trickle of water several

times before rejoining the Fossil Trail at 8.5 miles. Continue to the right, reaching the pavement in Big Sycamore Canyon at 8.6 miles.

From here, it is a steep 1.1 miles back up the road to your starting point. ■

Outcrop of volcanic rock on shoulder of Boney Mountain

Hike #47: Sandstone Peak

Distance	7 miles
Level of difficulty	Strenuous
Child rating	10 and up
Starting elevation	2050 feet
Highest point on trail	3111 feet
Topographic maps	Triunfo Pass, Newbury Park 7.5′
Guidebook map	23

The highest point in the Santa Monica Mountains, Sandstone Peak is not made of sandstone at all; it is a great prominence of volcanic rock, part of a large Miocene intrusion about 20 million years old that forms the spine of the range. The trail crosses chaparral-covered slopes, dips into an oak-lined creek corridor and ascends to the loftiest views on this part of the California coast.

To reach the trailhead, turn onto Yerba Buena Road from Highway 1 about 9 miles east of Point Mugu and 1 mile west of the Los Angeles-Ventura County line. Follow Yerba Buena Road 5 miles north to the Circle X Ranch ranger station, where maps and information are available, and then continue another mile to the Backbone Trail parking area on the left. The trail begins on the north side of the dirt parking area.

Description

Follow the dirt fire road north, climbing rather steeply up the brushy slope. The area was burned in the 1993 Greenmeadow Fire, but quickly recovered; only the blackened trunks of the larger shrubs and trees, charred but not consumed by the flames, serve as lasting reminders.

At 0.5 mile, the road reaches a signed junction with the Mishe Mokwa Trail. Follow this trail to the right, climb over a ridge and drop to another junction at 0.7 mile with a spur that leads back to another parking area on Yerba Buena Road. Go left, traveling northwest along the side of a canyon characterized by spectacularly weathered volcanic formations. The soil and rock are bright red, contrasting nicely with the subdued colors of the drought-resistant toyon, chamise, manzanita and yucca that blanket the slopes.

At 1.4 miles, keep an eye out on the opposite side of the canyon for Balanced Rock, a local landmark that quite obviously deserves its name. Beyond this point, the trail picks its way through a patch of boulders and descends to the Split Rock Picnic Area at 2.2 miles. Shaded by coast live oaks, California bay trees and sycamores, the rock is a huge boulder of volcanic breccia with a cleft in it broad enough to squeeze through. An unnamed stream supports the lush vegetation, including a healthy stand of poison oak, and its musical passage makes this a fine place to stop for lunch or a snack.

The trail crosses the creek and goes to the right past a rather sorry-looking picnic table. It climbs gently beyond the picnic area, then at 2.8 miles drops to cross a dry creekbed with interesting rock formations to either side.

At 3.4 miles the trail reaches a junction with a trail, now closed, that leads more directly to the top of Sandstone Peak. Continue on the broad main trail and descend to another junction at 3.8 miles. To the right, the Backbone Trail continues into the Boney Mountain Wilderness and Point Mugu State Park. Take the left fork and resume the steep ascent, reaching a junction at 4 miles with an unmarked spur that leads to a viewpoint on the right. At 4.1 miles you pass another spur to the right, this one leading to Inspiration Point at 2800 feet.

At 4.9 miles the climb grows steep and rocky, reaching a junction with another spur at 5 miles. This one ascends a series of stairs cut into the rock and then scrambles over a steep, exposed slope to the summit of Sandstone Peak, at 5.1 miles.

The summit is marked by a climbing register and a plaque identifying the peak as Mount Allen, named in honor of W. Herbert Allen, who donated the peak and surrounding property to the Boy Scouts of America in 1965. The ranch was purchased in 1986 by the Mountains Recreation and Conservation Authority, a joint local-state agency that in turn sold it to the National Park Service in 1987. A formal proposal to honor Allen's generosity by naming the peak after him had been submitted to the Department of the Interior, but the Board on Geographic Names has a long-standing policy of not naming landmarks after living individuals and it rejected the request. Local residents were undeterred, and posted the monument on the summit in 1969.

On a clear day, the 360-degree view from the peak is stunning, taking in the distant islands of San Clemente, Santa Catalina, Santa Barbara and San Nicolas, as well as the nearer northern Channel Islands of Anacapa, Santa Cruz, Santa Rosa and San Miguel. Inland, the views encompass the flat Oxnard Plain to the northwest and the distant Santa Ynez Mountains to the north.

After getting your fill of this one-of-a-kind view, retrace your steps to the main trail. Go right, ascend a slight rise and then begin the long downhill return. Fragments of asphalt underfoot show that the steep, switchbacking trail was once a paved road. At 6.5 miles the old road reaches the Mishe Mokwa trailhead; turn right and retrace your path to the parking area, which you reach at 7 miles. ∎

Hike #48: Satwiwa Loop

Distance	1.5 miles
Level of difficulty	Easy
Child rating	5 and up
Starting elevation	850 feet
Highest point on trail	1100 feet
Topographic map	Newbury Park 7.5′
Guidebook map	25

"Satwiwa" means "the bluffs" in the language of the Chumash, and it was the name of a village that once stood on the banks of a small stream in this corner of the Santa Monica Mountains. The property became part of the Santa Monica Mountains National Recreation Area in 1980; before that it was known as Rancho Sierra Vista, the name bestowed upon it by rancher Carl Beal, who had acquired it in 1937. It was originally part of the 48,672-acre Rancho El Conejo land grant deeded to former soldiers by the king of Spain.

In honor of its varied history, the property is now known as Rancho Sierra Vista/Satwiwa. It is home to the Satwiwa Native American Indian Culture Center, a visitor center that features programs and exhibits dedicated to the culture of the Chumash. A reconstructed native village, including a large circular dwelling constructed of reeds and logs, is nearby. The modern ranch buildings used by the last private owner have also been preserved, and are used by the Park Service to house rangers and maintenance facilities.

This easy loop trail leads past the village reconstruction and into the hills that surround the broad, rolling grassland. It serves as a fine introduction to Chumash culture and its relationship with the natural landscape.

The trailhead is at the Satwiwa visitor center. To reach it, follow Highway 101 to the west end of Thousand Oaks and take the Borchard Road exit. Follow Borchard south of the freeway to Reino Road, turn left and go 2 miles to Potrero Road. Turn right and follow Potrero a short distance to the sign indicating the entrance to Rancho Sierra Vista/Satwiwa. Park in the visitor lot and follow the road to the Culture Center.

The center is open 10 a.m. to 5 p.m. Saturday and Sunday, and offers a good selection of maps and books about the area. It also houses a small museum. Water and restrooms are available.

Description

The trail begins immediately south of the visitor center, next to the large reconstructed Chumash lodge. It leads gently uphill, heading east across the grassy hillside past a small pond frequented by waterfowl. In the distance, above and to the right, looms the volcanic outcropping of Boney Mountain. About 100 yards from the village site the trail forks. Bear right, crossing the drainage upstream of the pond and continuing through a field of ryegrass, vetch, poppies, wild radish, mustard and lupine.

At 0.3 mile you reach a junction. Take the center fork, heading toward a windmill visible on the hillside ahead. The trail climbs toward it along the course of an oak-shaded ravine that harbors a lush growth of poison oak.

At 0.4 mile the trail reaches a junction at the base of the windmill. Turn right, dropping back into the ravine and then climbing out the other side across a slope thick with laurel sumac and chamise. Blackened skeletons of oak trees indicate the path of a recent wildfire, the scars of which have mostly been erased.

The trail drops into another ravine at 0.6 mile and climbs out again. At 0.8 you reach another fork; go right. The trail ascends moderately through chaparral, bringing good views of the grassland below and the deeper cleft of Big Sycamore Canyon beyond, before beginning its gradual descent back toward the trailhead.

At 1.1 the trail reaches an intersection. Turn right and follow the trail about 20 yards to another junction. Take the center fork and follow the trail the remaining 0.4 mile back to the visitor center, visible to the north. ■

**Re-creation of a Chumash lodge
at Satwiwa Native American Indian Cultural Center**

Hike #49: Scenic Trail

Distance	4.3 miles
Level of difficulty	Moderate
Child rating	10 and up
Starting elevation	40 feet
Highest point on trail	1130 feet
Topographic map	Point Mugu 7.5'
Guidebook map	24

This hike climbs wildflower-covered slopes to a panoramic view of the Pacific and then winds along a sycamore-shaded creek. Although it gains 900 feet in elevation over the first 2 miles, the trail is well-engineered and the climb is not too demanding. Children younger than 10 can make it if the pace is slow and you stop often during the climb.

The trailhead is at the Sycamore Canyon Campground in Point Mugu State Park, 6 miles east of Point Mugu on the Pacific Coast Highway. Parking in the campground costs $6 a day, but there are dirt pullouts alongside the highway where you can park for free. Follow the road north through the campground to a locked gate, where the trail begins.

Description

Hike about 20 yards past the gate and turn left at a sign that marks the start of the Scenic Trail. Crossing Sycamore Creek, the trail passes through a rich stand of poison oak and begins climbing at 0.1 mile. This area was burned in the 1993 Greenmeadow Fire, but the vegetation quickly recovered and the slope is covered by laurel sumac, Spanish broom and paintbrush.

The well-used trail crosses a largely open hillside with good views back into the canyon and to the ocean, and reaches a junction at 0.3 mile. Go straight. At 0.4 mile the ascent grows easier, and at 0.8 mile the trail reaches a junction in a saddle. To the left and straight ahead are trails that lead out to the edge of the ridge and prominent viewpoints. The main trail continues to the right, following the sign directing you to the Overlook Trail.

A few yards farther you reach another junction. Go right, heading north to an intersection at 1 mile with the Overlook Trail, a dirt road open to mountain bikes. Go left, following the road northwest and enjoying good views of distant Boney Peak.

The trail continues climbing for the next mile through dry terrain, where yucca and prickly-pear cactus dominate. At 2 miles you reach a signed junction atop the ridge. Turn right and follow the crest of the ridge downhill toward the

Big Sycamore Canyon Trail. The moderate descent across a grassy slope steepens at 2.2 miles, and at 2.3 miles the trail curves north and begins a series of long, gentle switchbacks down the side of a ravine.

The trail meets the floor of Sycamore Canyon at 3.5 miles. Go right and follow the canyon downhill toward the ocean, passing the Overlook Trail junction at 3.8 miles and reaching the start of the Scenic Trail at 4.3 miles. ■

Hike #50: Serrano Valley

Distance	3.2 miles
Level of difficulty	Easy
Child rating	5 and up
Starting elevation	1000 feet
Lowest point on trail	375 feet
Topographic map	Triunfo Pass 7.5′
Guidebook map	26

Serrano Valley is a seldom-visited bowl encircled by rugged cliffs and steep slopes in Boney Mountain State Wilderness. This easy trail follows the route of an abandoned road through a luxuriant grassland to the site of a farmstead long since consumed by wildfire. It is a pleasant walk in springtime when the grass is still green and the wildflowers are in bloom.

To reach the trailhead take Highway 1, the Pacific Coast Highway, to Deer Creek Road, which is about 3 miles west of the Ventura County-Los Angeles County Line. Follow this road — which becomes Pacific View Road and then Cothrain Road — 4.6 miles as it climbs steeply into the mountains. This drive alone makes the trip worthwhile, for it offers spectacular views of the Pacific Ocean, the shoreline and the northern Channel Islands.

Turn left onto Serrano Valley Road, which is extremely narrow and steep, and drive 1 mile to the locked gate. Space is tight here, so turn around carefully and pull as far onto the shoulder as you can.

The trail follows the abandoned road past the gate. There are no restrooms or water at the trailhead.

Description

The moderately steep trail switchbacks downhill across chaparral-covered hillside into Serrano Valley, which is visible to the west. Atop the steep north wall of the valley are spectacular volcanic outcroppings, forming a craggy escarpment. At 0.5 mile the trail crosses a small, shady creekbed and begins winding through rolling grasslands on the valley floor.

At 0.75 mile the trail dips into a small gully and climbs out the other side, reaching a fork at 1 mile. A faint trail climbs into the hills to the right; stay left and follow the main trail through the tall grass toward a fence line about 50 yards ahead that marks the boundary of Boney Mountain State Wilderness Area.

At 1.3 miles the trail crosses another gully and leads past a grove of canyon oaks before crossing another fence line at 1.5 miles. A pair of concrete pillars here mark the entrance to the grounds of the former ranch house, of which only a few scattered remnants — rusting farm equipment, broken pipes, blackened trees, derelict furnishings — remain. The home site is at 1.6 miles.

According to old maps, a trail once led from here and looped around the rest of the valley, connecting with a route through Serrano Canyon and on into Big Sycamore Canyon to the west. The route has become overgrown through disuse, however, and would require cross-country bushwhacking to follow. Newer maps do not depict it.

From the home site, a number of newer dwellings are visible on the steep ridges to the south and east. Despite poor access and the constant threat of wildfire, people seeking solitude and spectacular views are willing to spend enormous sums of money to develop this rugged land. This encroachment offers proof of the need to set aside tracts of the mountains to serve as havens for wildlife and as buffers against urbanization.

Return the way you came. ∎

Recommended Reading

Bakker, Elna. *An Island Called California*. Berkeley: University of California Press, 1984.

Beck, Warren A., and Haase, Ynez D. *Historical Atlas of California*. Norman: University of Oklahoma Press, 1974.

Belzer, Thomas J. *Roadside Plants of Southern California*. Missoula: Mountain Press Publishing Co., 1984.

Burtness, Bob. *A Camper's Guide to the Tri-County Area*. Santa Barbara: Mission Council, Boy Scouts of America, 1984.

California Coastal Commission. *California Coastal Access Guide*. Berkeley: University of California Press, 1991.

Clarke, Herbert. *An Introduction to Southern California Birds*. Missoula, Montana: Mountain Press Publishing Co., 1989.

Dale, Nancy. *Flowering Plants of the Santa Monica Mountains*. Santa Barbara: Capra Press, 1986.

Darville, Fred T. Jr. *Mountaineering Medicine: A Wilderness Medical Guide*. 14th edition. Berkeley: Wilderness Press, 1997.

Dowty, Karen Jones. *A Visitor's Guide: The California Channel Islands*. Ventura: The Boxwood Press, 1981.

Gibson, Robert O. *The Chumash*. New York: Chelsea House Publishers, 1991.

Glassow, Michael A. *Purisimeño Chumash Prehistory: Maritime Adaptations Along the Southern California Coast*. New York: Harcourt Brace College Publishers, 1996.

——, ed. *Archaeology on the Northern Channel Islands of California: Studies in Subsistence, Economics and Social Organization*. Salinas: Coyote Press, 1993.

Heizer, R.F., and Whipple, M.A. *The California Indians: A Source Book*. Berkeley: University of California Press, 1971.

Hudson, Travis, and Underhay, Ernest. *Crystals in the Sky: An Intellectual Odyssey Involving Chumash Astronomy, Cosmology and Rock Art*. Santa Barbara: Ballena Press, 1978.

Kroeber, A.L. *Handbook of the Indians of California*. New York: Dover Publications, 1976.

Lester, Elizabeth Sherman. *The Legendary King of San Miguel*. Santa Barbara: McNally & Loftin, 1974.

McConnaughey, Bayard H., and McConnaughey, Evelyn. *Pacific Coast: A National Audubon Society Nature Guide*. New York: Alfred A. Knopf, 1985.

McElrath, Clifford. *On Santa Cruz Island*. Santa Barbara: Santa Barbara Historical Society, 1993.

Power, Dennis, editor. *The California Islands: Proceedings of a Multidisciplinary Symposium*. Santa Barbara: Santa Barbara Museum of Natural History, 1980.

Ricketts, Edward F., Calvin, Jack, and Hedgpeth, Joel W. *Between Pacific Tides*. Fifth edition, revised by David W. Phillips. Stanford: Stanford University Press, 1985.

Roberts, Lois J. *San Miguel Island, Santa Barbara's Fourth Island West*. Carmel: Cal Rim Books, 1991.

Sharp, Robert P., and Glazner, Allen F. *Geology Underfoot in Southern California*. Missoula: Mountain Press Publishing Co., 1993.

Wieman, Harold. *Nature Walks on the San Luis Coast*. Arroyo Grande: Bear Flag Books, 1980.

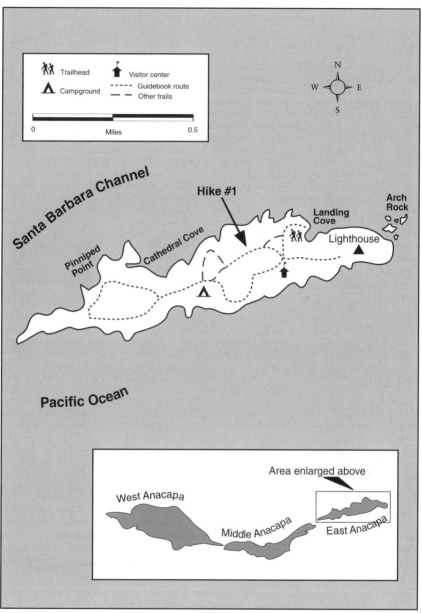

Map 1. Anacapa Island (Hike 1)

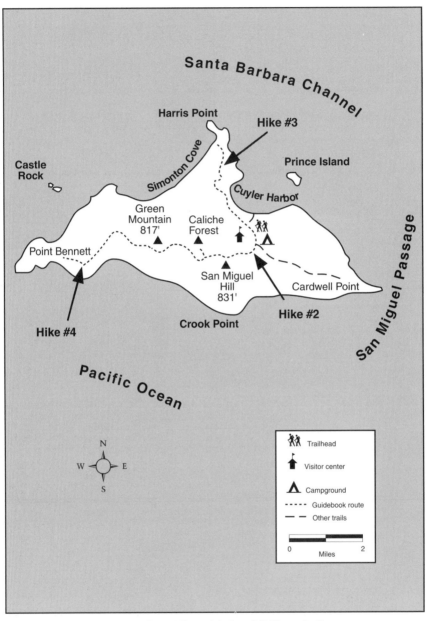

Map 2. San Miguel Island (Hikes 2-4)

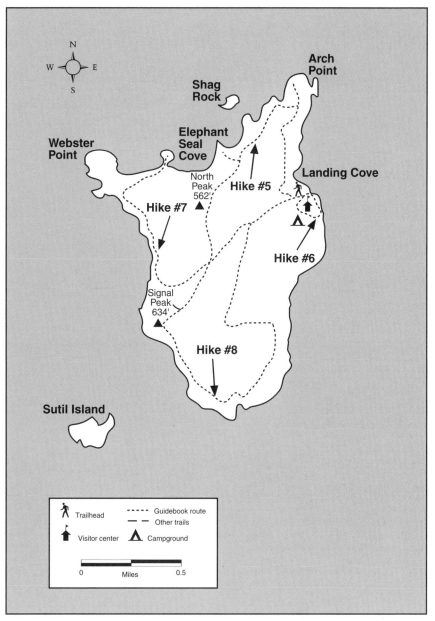

Map 3. Santa Barbara Island (Hikes 5-8)

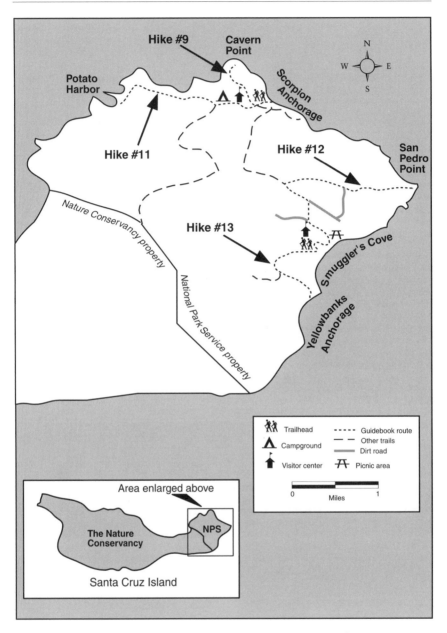

Map 4. Santa Cruz Island (Hikes 9, 11–13)

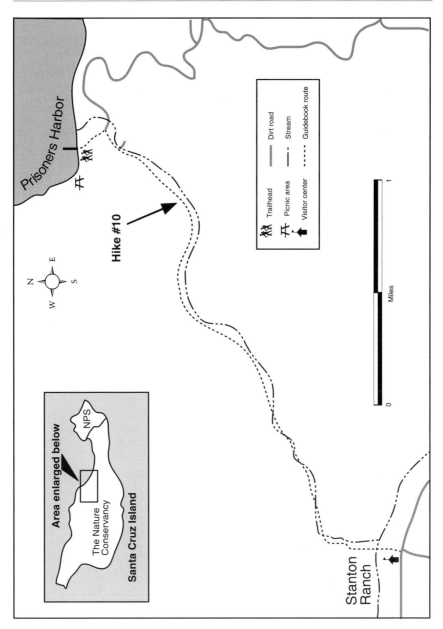

Map 5. Santa Cruz Island (Hike 10)

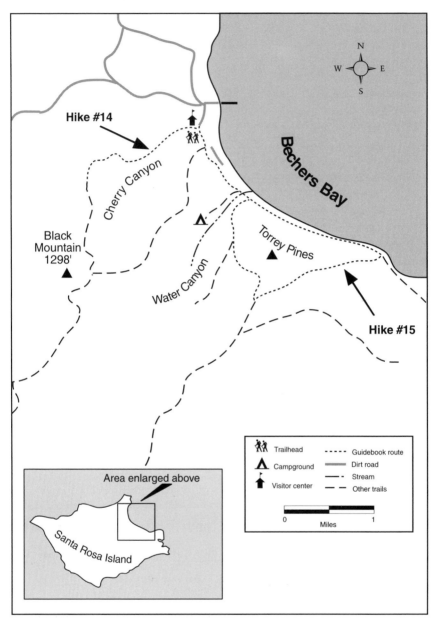

Map 6. Santa Rosa Island (Hikes 14, 15)

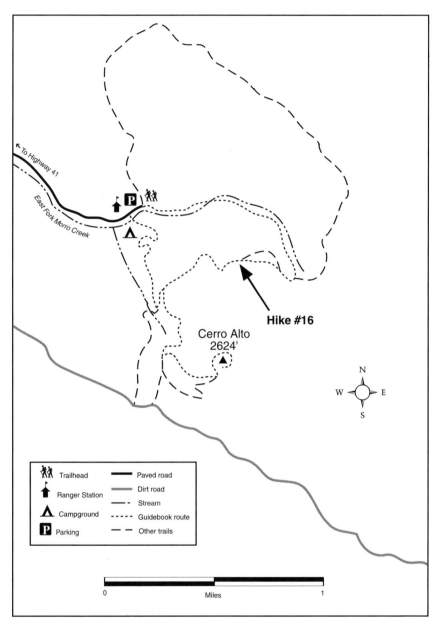

Map 7. Los Padres (Hike 16)

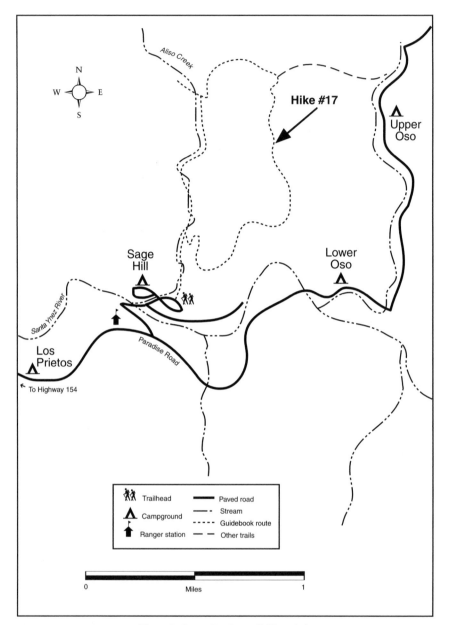

Map 8. Los Padres (Hike 17)

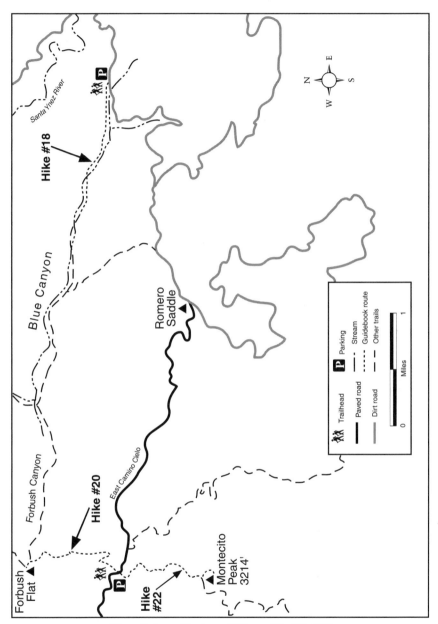

Map 9. Los Padres (Hikes 18, 20, 22)

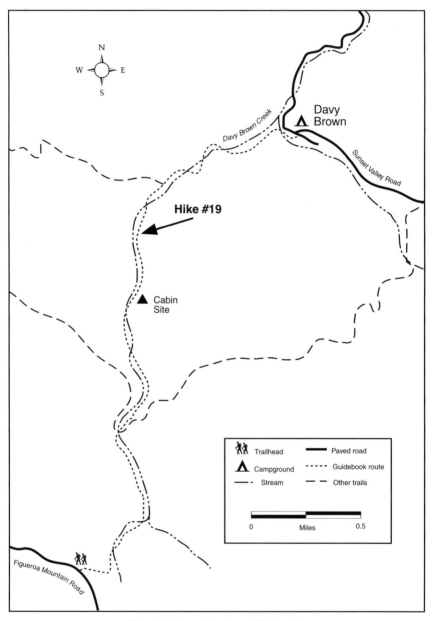

Map 10. Los Padres (Hike 19)

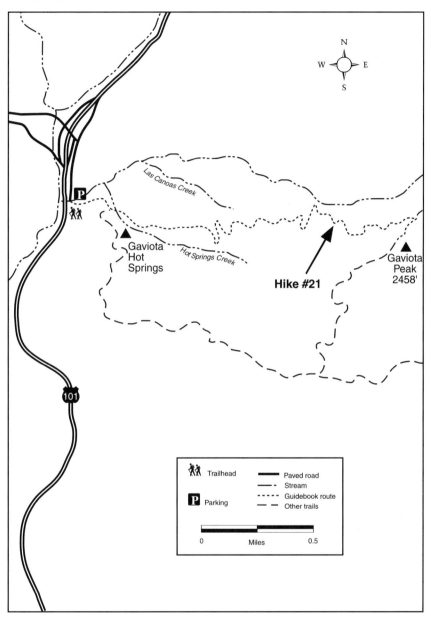

Map 11. Los Padres (Hike 21)

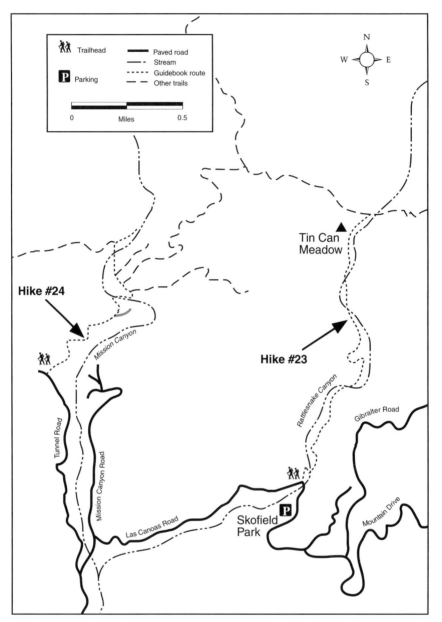

Map 12. Los Padres (Hikes 23, 24)

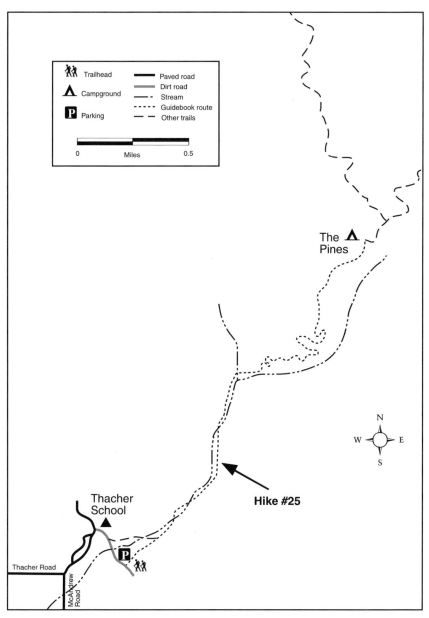

Map 13. Los Padres (Hike 25)

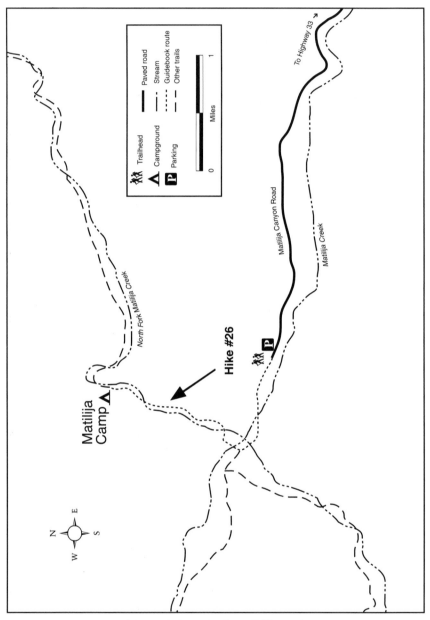

Map 14. Los Padres (Hike 26)

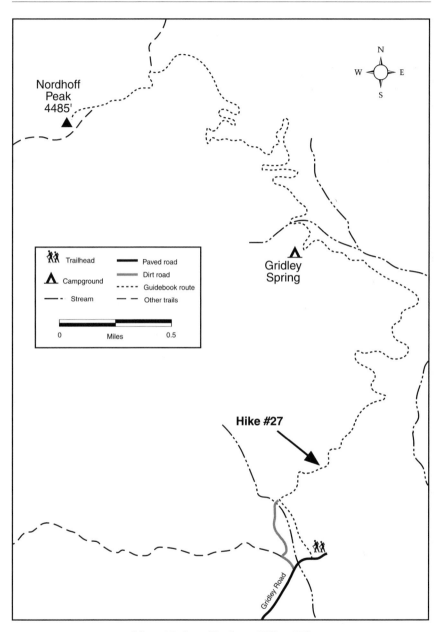

Map 15. Los Padres (Hike 27)

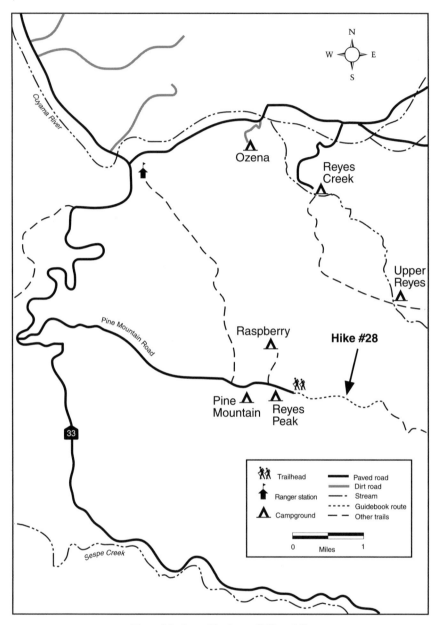

Map 16. Los Padres (Hike 28)

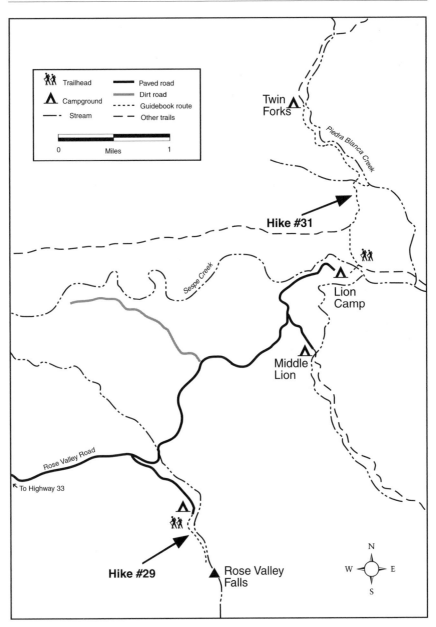

Map 17. Los Padres (Hikes 29, 31)

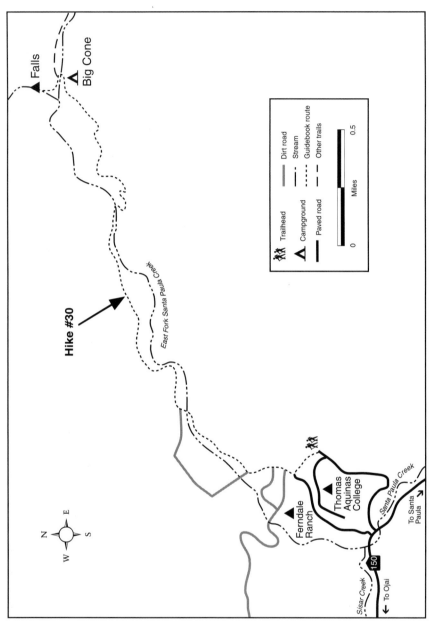

Map 18. Los Padres (Hike 30)

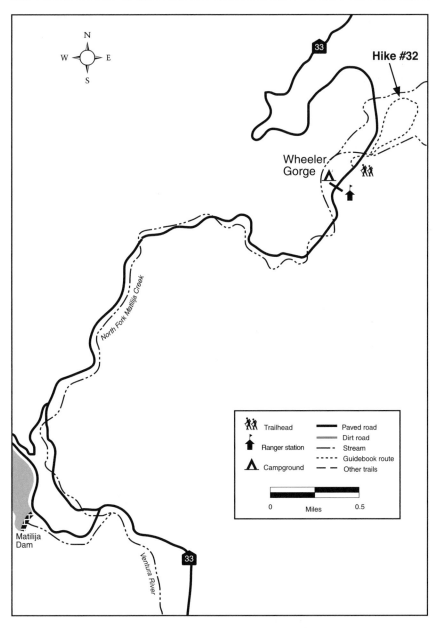

Map 19. Los Padres (Hike 32)

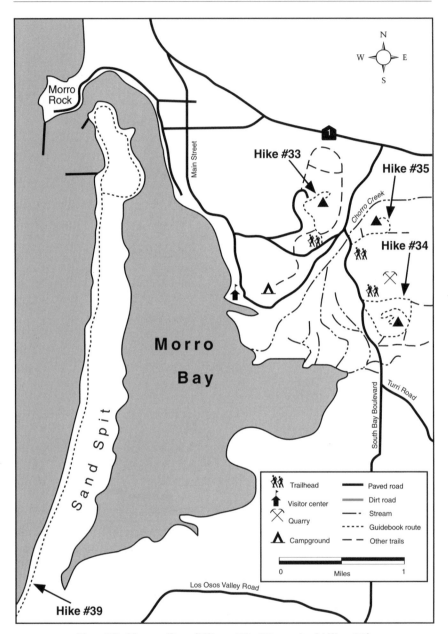

Map 20. Morro Bay (Hikes 33–35, end of Hike 39)

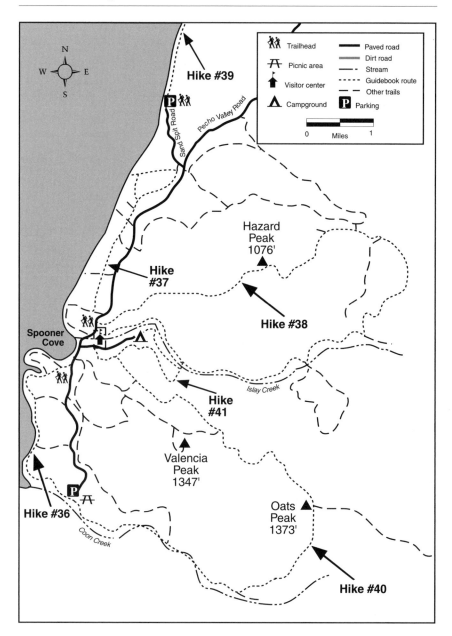

Map 21. Montaña de Oro (Hikes 36–38, start of Hike 39, Hikes 40–41)

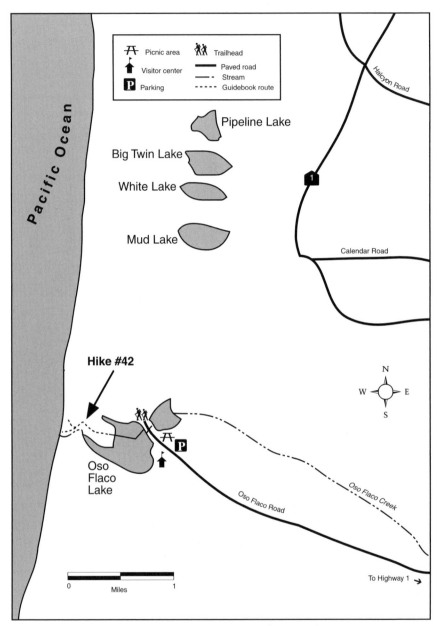

Map 22. Nipomo Dunes (Hike 42)

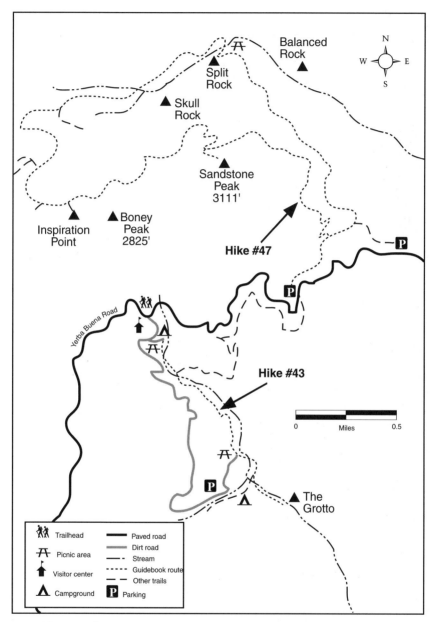

Map 23. Santa Monica Mountains National Recreation Area
(Hikes 43, 47)

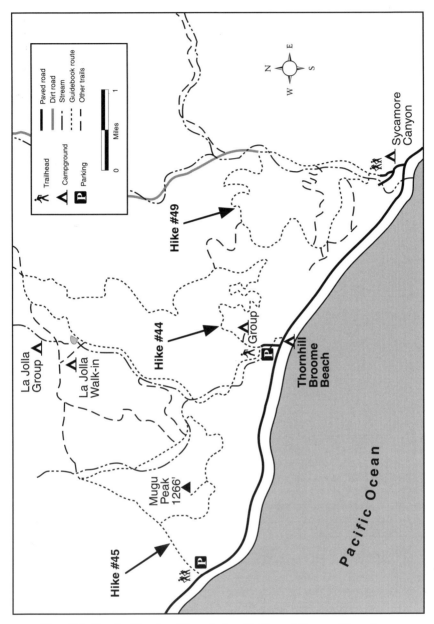

**Map 24. Santa Monica Mountains National Recreation Area
(Hikes 44–45, 49)**

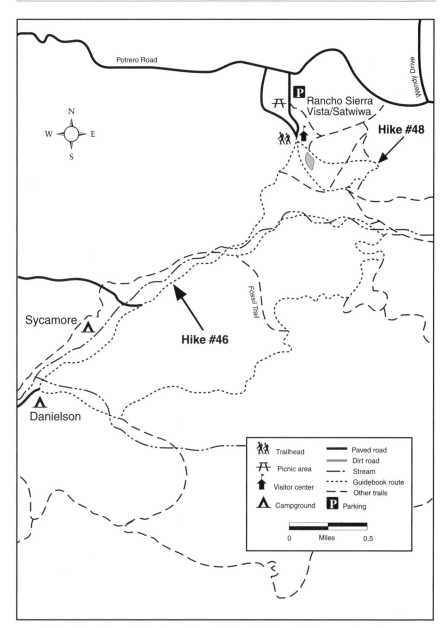

**Map 25. Santa Monica Mountains National Recreation Area
(Hikes 46, 48)**

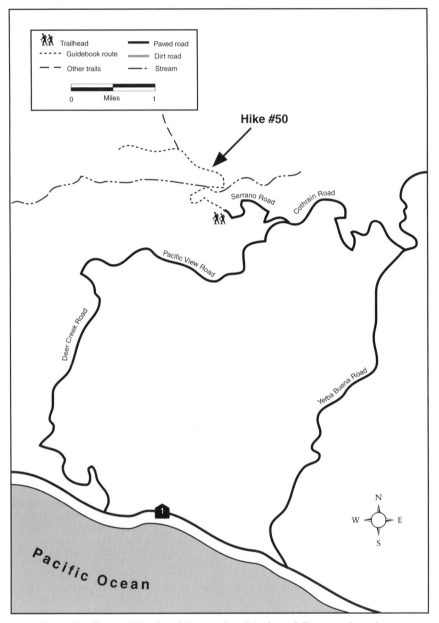

Map 25. Santa Monica Mountains National Recreation Area
(Hike 50)

Index

Page numbers in *italics* indicate photographs